"Frei and Morriss have written the definitive guide to leadership today, just when we need it most. In voices that are fresh, playful, and unapologetically direct, they give us permission to look beyond ourselves and focus instead on the true challenge of leadership: how to help others unlock their full potential."

—**ARIANNA HUFFINGTON,** founder and CEO, Thrive Global

"Through insight drawn from their extensive work teaching leaders and companies how to thrive, Frances Frei and Anne Morriss offer more proof that trust is a competitive advantage and the key to building effective, happy teams."

—**DOUG MCMILLON,** President and CEO, Walmart

"No matter where you are on your leadership journey, the engaging stories and real-life examples Frei and Morriss use to illustrate the traits of effective leaders will help you empower others to do their best work and create lasting impact."

—**PEGGY JOHNSON,** Executive Vice President, Business Development, Microsoft

"The only way to scale a company is to apply the ideas in this guide and be a leader whose success is ultimately in the decisions and actions of your teams."

—**JEN WONG,** Chief Operating Officer, Reddit

"Talking about love at work isn't normal yet, but it should be. Love is fundamental to happiness and productivity at work. This book is a powerful resource for any leader who aspires to be most effective in our emerging future."

—**MIGUEL MCKELVEY,** cofounder and Chief Culture Officer, WeWork

"Frei and Morriss have a unique gift of understanding how to empower leaders to unlock the potential in themselves, their teams, and their businesses. The guidance they share in *Unleashed* is invaluable for me and for the leadership teams I work with."

—**JACQUI CANNEY,** Chief People Officer, WPP

"In *Unleashed*, Frei and Morriss provide an incredibly compelling case for effective leadership by distilling what leadership is all about. The stories and frameworks have helped me take meaningful steps on my lifelong journey toward being a better person and a better leader."

—**MARC MERRILL,** cofounder and Cochairman, Riot Games

"Frei and Morriss have brilliantly encapsulated what normally takes a leader many years and many mistakes to learn and have given it back to the reader in the form of a beautiful blueprint for successful leadership. *Unleashed* is full of relevant experiences I wish I'd had when I moved from leading individuals to leading teams—and realized it was no longer about me."

—**JENNIFER MORGAN,** Co-CEO and Member of the Executive Board, SAP

"The first step to breakthrough is self-realization. The next step is harnessing the career-catapulting lessons in *Unleashed*."

—**BOZOMA SAINT JOHN,** Chief Marketing Officer, Endeavor

UNLEASHED

The Unapologetic Leader's Guide to Empowering Everyone Around You

FRANCES FREI & ANNE MORRISS

Harvard Business Review Press • Boston, Massachusetts

HBR Press Quantity Sales Discounts

Harvard Business Review Press titles are available at significant quantity discounts when purchased in bulk for client gifts, sales promotions, and premiums. Special editions, including books with corporate logos, customized covers, and letters from the company or CEO printed in the front matter, as well as excerpts of existing books, can also be created in large quantities for special needs.

For details and discount information for both print and ebook formats, contact booksales@harvardbusiness.org, tel. 800-988-0886, or www.hbr.org/bulksales.

The web addresses referenced in this book were live and correct at the time of the book's publication but may be subject to change.

Library of Congress Cataloging-in-Publication Data

Names: Frei, Frances, author. | Morriss, Anne, author.
Title: Unleashed : the unapologetic leader's guide to empowering everyone
    around you / Frances Frei, Anne Morriss.
Description: Boston, MA : Harvard Business Review Press, [2020] | Includes
    index.
Identifiers: LCCN 2020000145 (print) | LCCN 2020000146 (ebook) | ISBN
    9781633697041 (hardcover) | ISBN 9781633697058 (ebook)
Subjects: LCSH: Employee empowerment. | Executive ability. |
    Executives—Psychology. | Leadership.
Classification: LCC HD50.5 .F73 2020 (print) | LCC HD50.5 (ebook) | DDC
    658.3/14—dc23
LC record available at https://lccn.loc.gov/2020000145
LC ebook record available at https://lccn.loc.gov/2020000146

ISBN: 978-1-63369-704-1
eISBN: 978-1-63369-705-8

The paper used in this publication meets the requirements of the American National Standard for Permanence of Paper for Publications and Documents in Libraries and Archives Z39.48-1992.

FOR ALEC AND BEN,
May the best of you be unbound,
and may you taste the sacred joy
of setting other people free.

Just remember that your real job is that if you are free, you need to free somebody else. If you have some power, then your job is to empower somebody else.

—TONI MORRISON,
as quoted in *O, The Oprah Magazine*

CONTENTS

PART TWO

ABSENCE

UNLEASHED

1

IT'S NOT ABOUT YOU

There are *a lot* of books about leadership, many of them terrific. Humans have been dwelling on the practice and mystery of great leadership for millennia (more on that later). Why read one more? Well, if you look around, it's clear that many of the existing models of leadership are not wholly up to the task of handling the challenges we now face together. From rebuilding trust in institutions to unleashing potential at the scale of organizations and beyond, we believe that traditional ideas about leadership only get us so far. They carry us through the first few miles of today's leadership marathon, but often set us up to lose momentum before we get all the way to the finish line of impact.[a]

The problem, respectfully, is that it's been all about *you*. Your talents and shortcomings as a leader. Your confidence and lack of it. Your heroic moments of courage and instinct—and, of course, your epic falls from grace. For all kinds of good reasons, including the demands of good storytelling, traditional leadership narratives

a. This is the first of a number of awkward sports analogies.

assume that the vision-having, strategy-making, troops-rallying leader is the most important person in the scene.

In this book, we propose a different orientation. Our starting point is that leadership, at its core, isn't about you. Instead, it's about how effective you are at empowering *other* people and unleashing *their* full potential. And we will begin by making the case that if you seek to lead, then the important work ahead starts with turning outward.

Consider these questions: Are your teammates and colleagues better off when you're around? Are they more productive and more engaged? More willing to innovate and take smart bets? Whatever your answers are, hold on to them as we begin this conversation. The response we hear most often is "sometimes," and it's the typical pattern we observe among even the most seasoned leaders. Leaders of all backgrounds and tenures only sometimes succeed in creating conditions that allow other people to thrive, and few have full control over the levers of their success. Our mission here is to help you fix that.

Who do we think we are?

We are scholars and writers, coaches and company builders, optimists and (on our best days) accelerators of action. It has been the privilege of our lives to work as change agents at some of the world's most influential organizations—companies like Uber, WeWork and Riot Games—and with some of the world's most inspiring business leaders, people like Jen Morgan at SAP, Doug McMillon at Walmart, and Bozoma Saint John at, well, any room she decides to walk into. But at the core of our identities, we are educators, which is why we wanted to write a book about leadership. We believe that what we've learned in the process of changing things can be useful to anyone who seeks to lead, particularly now, when the scale and complexity of our shared challenges can seem overwhelming. We believe that our highest duty is to current and future generations of leaders who are willing to put themselves out there and try to build a better world.

We were both taken by the idea of leadership at a curiously young age. Frances first became interested in the context of sports: how coaches helped players reach their potential, how players made *each other* better on and off the court, how the joy and heartbreak of competition seemed to elevate everyone in the game. For Anne, oddly enough, it turned into an obsession with the American Revolution at the delicate age of nine. Side effects included regular appearances as a cross-dressed minuteman and middle-of-the-night reenactments of Paul Revere's ride.[b] We were not like the other kids.

In both of these arenas, it was the poetic, often breathtaking acts of leadership that captured our early imagination: Michael Jordan's embodiment of excellence in his dazzling drives to the basket, John Adams's willingness to defend enemy soldiers in court, on principles that would inspire the best version of a new nation. These were people who seemed to defy the limits of their humanity in pursuit of something bigger than themselves. Their example expanded possibilities for anyone paying attention, even centuries later, even for two wide-eyed and slack-jawed little girls who had no real business dreaming of living outsized lives.

We assumed to be a leader meant to "Be Like Mike," which seemed like a highly unlikely prospect. As we both started playing sports ourselves—and starting revolutions, in our own small ways—we discovered leadership was a lot messier (and less beautiful to watch) than we had imagined. It wasn't only about the guy

---

b. She once woke up her siblings, wild-eyed and *sleepwalking*, with shouts of "the British are coming!"

flying through the air, but also about—indeed, *primarily* about—what everyone else on the court was doing.

As we went on to study organizations and build them, we discovered that the daily work of leading is much quieter and less dramatic than the leadership stories that had captivated us as children. That kind of work happens in the honest conversation with a colleague who's not meeting your expectations or in the decision to take a chance on someone who's not sure they're ready for the job. It happens in the long walk to your boss's office to tell them that you've looked at the data from every possible angle and their strategy isn't working. The practice of leadership almost always asks you to risk something, but it only sometimes requires a midnight ride or a clutch, buzzer-beating jump shot. And there's rarely a crowd that goes wild when you get it right.

A new definition of leadership

We have dedicated our lives to making leaders and organizations better. Here's the important, intuition-bending leadership principle that this experience has taught us: the real work of leadership isn't particularly concerned with the leader. It isn't so worried about the speechifying person at the front of the room. Whether they're loved or feared. How smart they sound. Whether their rival is becoming too powerful. Yes, those things can end up mattering around the edges, but they are sideshows to leadership's genuine ringmaster. Again, leadership, at its core, isn't about you. It's about how effective you are at unleashing *other people*. Full stop. That's it. That's the secret.

The practical definition of leadership we use in our work is that *leadership is about empowering other people as a result of your presence—and making sure that impact continues into your absence.*[1]

Your job as a leader is to create the conditions for the people around you to become increasingly effective, to help them fully realize their own capacity and power. And not only when you're in the trenches with them, but also when you're not around, and even (this is the cleanest test) after you've permanently moved on from the team.

This orientation becomes more important as your leadership mandate grows. When Stacy Brown-Philpot, now the CEO of TaskRabbit (more to come on Brown-Philpot) went from managing a fourteen-person team to ultimately more than a thousand, she realized she had to rethink her approach to leadership.[2] For context, Brown-Philpot was working at Google at the time, where she was already well known as a strategic, results-oriented leader. She was in the process of rocketing to the top of Sheryl Sandberg's operations organization, pausing to launch the Black Googlers Network along the way. Brown-Philpot had gone to Sandberg with the observation that black professionals were underrepresented at Google—and the conviction that a dedicated effort to recruit, retain, and connect them to each other would make a difference. Sandberg challenged Brown-Philpot to lead the effort herself: "You're it. You're the person that you've been waiting for to do this."[3]

Brown-Philpot already was, to use a technical term, a rock star. And yet she found herself walking out of meetings with her direct reports, incredibly frustrated. The way she tells the story, she would show up with her own agenda—a list of the "ten things" she wanted to accomplish—and after only getting through one of them in the course of the meeting, she would code the interaction a leadership failure. Her breakthrough came when she reframed her purpose: "What I needed to learn . . . was that this meeting is not about you, Stacy. This meeting is about the person that you're leading."[4] As Brown-Philpot describes it, she shifted her focus going forward from what *she* needed to be successful as a leader to what she needed to do to help *others* succeed. This reframing has powered her to the

Ten Signs It Might Be All about You

Leadership requires you to be present to the needs, abilities, and potential of other people—and to respond quickly and strategically to those signals. When it's all about you, all of the time, that's virtually impossible to do. Here are some warning signs that you may be getting in your own way as a leader and making a habit out of self-distraction:

1. **What other people experience rarely occurs to you.** The path to empowering other people starts with curiosity about what they're thinking, feeling, and doing. If you find yourself focused primarily on your own experience, then you're still a healthy distance from the emotional launchpad of leadership.

2. **You don't ask very many questions.** A measurable indicator of your interest in others is the number of questions you ask them or at least *want* to ask them. If this isn't an impulse you feel very often, then you may be stuck in your own head. The good news is that the remedy is actionable (get in there, inquiring minds!), and there's a prize inside for going for it: people tend to become more interesting as you learn more about them.

3. **The most interesting thing about other people is what they think of you.** We all care what other people think about us. This is different from caring so much that you're disinterested in all the *other* thoughts someone else might be having. If you can't sustain genuine interest in the ideas of other people, including those ideas that have nothing to do with you, then you haven't yet earned the right to lead.

4. **You're constantly updating a catalogue of your own weaknesses, limitations, and imperfections.** A loud inner critic can

be a major distraction from the practice of leadership. Take our friend Arianna Huffington's advice and evict that obnoxious roommate from inside your head, the one spinning negative stories about you out of dubious data.

5. **Other people's abilities bum you out.** When you're in an effective leadership state, the strengths and potential of the people around you become your greatest assets. If your primary response to other people's capabilities is to feel worse about your own, then you probably need a healthy time-out from the leadership path. Do what it takes to nourish yourself (and stay off Instagram).

6. **You're constantly in crisis.** The human experience is fraught with moments that require immediate, unwavering attention to self—also known as "crises." There's no quota for how many of these you get to have in a month, year, or lifetime, but if your numbers are way above your peers', then you're probably not well positioned to lead them.

7. **You're pessimistic about the future.** Leadership is built on the assumption that tomorrow can be better than today. If you have a hard time buying into such a romantic idea, if you dismiss it along with rainbows and unicorns, then we suggest you try your hand at something else. Despair is the opposite of leadership.

8. **Reality has become tedious.** When you're regularly practicing leadership, the world is a pretty magical place, filled with progress to be made and human potential to be unleashed. It's

(continued)

a red flag if it's been awhile since you've felt a sense of wonder at the unlimited possibilities around you.

9. **Apathy and powerlessness are dominant emotions.** You may have come by these feelings very honestly, but leadership asks you to be in touch with your own agency and ability to influence your surroundings. It asks you to know your own power so—among other things—you can introduce other people to theirs. If you're not feeling it, for whatever reason, then you won't be to able pull this off.

10. **You're the star of your own show.** If this sentence can be used to describe the way you move through the world, then you're not in the leadership game. Period. Those of us hungry for leadership will eventually change the channel.

very top of the tech industry, a place where it's not so easy to find a woman of color in senior leadership.

If we look at leadership from this perspective, then it's less about what the C-suite is up to at any given moment and more about what the rest of the company is doing. A leader's charge is less about the decisions that happen to cross their desk and more about the decisions that don't even make it into the building. Leaders must be intentional about distributing power and decision rights, and then take total, unqualified responsibility for the outcome. Other people are making judgment calls all day, every day—and your job is to make sure that they're getting it right, that their choices reflect the vision, values, and strategy of the organization. (See the sidebar "Ten Signs It Might Be All about You.")

In other words, a leader's mission is to ensure that everyone on the team—wherever they may be—has a fighting chance at wild success. This has arguably always been true, but it is certainly true now, as our challenges become larger in scale, faster to mutate, and grislier in their complexity than ever before. Leaders today need to spend less time checking their teeth in the mirror and more time getting other people to pull up their socks.

The leadership pivot

Whenever we share our all-about-you warning signs, we find that most leaders can relate to at least a few of them. To be clear, if you saw yourself anywhere on that list, it doesn't disqualify you from leadership (we've all become stars of our own show at some point). But it does mean you may be able to improve as a leader if you start thinking more about how to empower other people.

For a good example of what we're talking about, watch Reid Hoffman in action. Hoffman was cofounder and executive chairman of LinkedIn—among the most successful entrepreneurs on the planet—and is also one of the most empowering leaders we've ever observed. Hoffman founded LinkedIn after helping to build PayPal, and now shares his capital, wisdom, and infectious brand of optimism across multiple platforms. Hoffman put it this way: "As a leader, you have to constantly shut off your own reel and watch all the movies playing around you."[5]

We love the movie metaphor. In fact, the central questions of leadership have little to do with your own performance as a leader (how'd I do?) and almost everything to do with the performance of others (how'd *they* do?). Figure 1-1 is the visual translation of your mission as a leader: to continuously improve the performance of the people around you.

FIGURE 1-1

Leadership performance curve

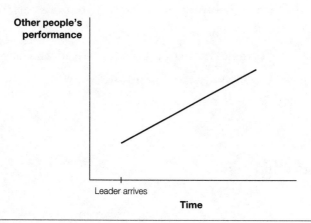

Try drawing your own leadership performance curve. Recall a team you've been on, one where you've spent some real time (no less than three months). What happened to the slope of *other people's* performance after you showed up? Did it go up or down? If your curve generally looks like the one in the figure, then you (likely) helped to create the conditions for other people to succeed. But if it's flat or negative or simply not as steep as you know was possible, think back to the choices you made as a leader and teammate. What could you have done—big or small—to improve your team's performance?

The purpose of this thought exercise is to start taking radical responsibility for the experiences of other people, which is the decision at the heart of empowerment leadership. Of course, there are things that can impact performance that have nothing to do with you, externalities that may be outside your control (e.g., a competitor moves in next door). The point is to gain insight from the idea, however delusional you think it may be, that it all came down to your ability to create the conditions where other people could perform. If this level of accountability feels uncomfortable and unreasonable, then you're doing the exercise correctly.

What more could you have done to unleash the people around you? As we will suggest many times in the chapters ahead, activate your best thinking by writing down your answers. We've taken thousands of executives through this exercise, and the piece of paper in front of them is never blank. We've all missed opportunities for leadership impact, all of us, for one reason or another. Here's where it usually gets interesting: *Why?* Why did you miss the chance to fully empower another person or team or organization?

The answer we hear most often is that you made it somehow about you. You turned inward rather than outward, directing energy toward your own hopes and fears, rather than those of your team. As Hoffman might say, you couldn't figure out how to turn off your own movie.

Here's an example: for some of us, the decision to lead has sometimes felt too presumptuous or risky. It can take courage to own your ability to make something better, and there can be financial or political costs in refusing to accept the status quo. If you have a pattern of hesitating in the face of leadership opportunity, we suggest spending some time with the pattern. What held you back?

Full disclosure: we're not all that interested in the details of your answer—this is your own backstory, which we assume is filled with rational, hard-earned choices. We are, however, deeply invested in the trade-offs of these choices and in removing any barriers to your impact in the world. The truth is that we're all susceptible to prioritizing security, incredibly helpful in getting us through the day, to say nothing of surviving the human experience. If your objective is to lead, however, then you'll eventually need to give up some of that security, at least some of the time.

Our advice is to follow Hoffman's lead and risk making other people the heroes of your leadership story. Sometimes protecting ourselves is the right choice, but we're often unreliable calculators of personal risk and return. In our experience, most people can handle far more exposure than they think they can—and almost everyone underestimates the meaning that leadership brings to their lives. In exchange for the anxiety of flying without a net, you get to travel to unimaginable places.

If your objective is to lead, then unleashing other people—helping them become as effective as they can possibly be—is your fundamental mandate. Rather than threatening your own primacy, other people's excellence becomes the truest measure of your success, your way to go faster and farther than you ever could on your own. That's the transformative impact of empowerment leadership.

Empowerment leadership

It all starts, we believe, with trust. Trust creates the conditions for other people to be guided by you, which is the focus of chapter 2. It's the work you need to do on *yourself* before other people will take a leadership leap of faith with you. Once you do that work, you then earn the right to have impact on others at progressively greater scale.

We summarize this worldview in figure 1-2, which also provides the structure for the book. The idea is that as you move outward from the foundational *trust* bull's-eye (chapter 2), you gain the skills to empower more and more people, from individuals (via *love*, chapter 3) to teams (via *belonging*, chapter 4) to organizations (via *strategy*, chapter 5) and even beyond (via *culture*, chapter 6). This is our take on what we call empowerment leadership, and it's the ride we'll go on together over the course of this book.

In other words, the first step on the leadership path—once you can reliably build trust—is to create a context where the people around you can thrive. This requires you to set high standards and reveal deep devotion at the same time, a nontrivial challenge we call

FIGURE 1-2

Rings of empowerment leadership

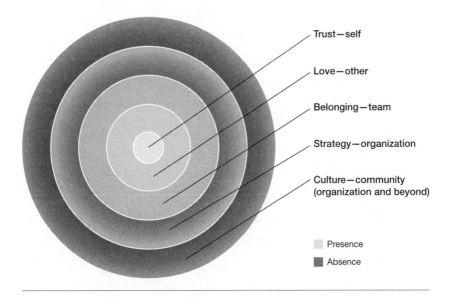

Trust—self

Love—other

Belonging—team

Strategy—organization

Culture—community
(organization and beyond)

Presence

Absence

love and the idea we explore in chapter 3. To create a context where *teams* thrive, however, requires something more. Leading a team with any type of difference embedded in it (and we will argue that this describes most teams) requires you to champion that difference and ensure that everyone can contribute their unique capacities and perspectives. This is the essence of belonging and the theme of chapter 4.

Mastering trust, love, and belonging—the core competencies of empowerment leadership—is an extraordinary achievement. But practicing them requires you to be present for the action (or at least not missing from it for long) and limits your impact to the people you can directly influence. The most successful leaders are influencing people far beyond their direct reach and intensely aware that success depends on what happens in their absence. Which brings us to the outer rings of our model: strategy and culture. Strategy and culture are invisible forces that shape organizations and empower other people whether or not you happen to be present. If you seek to lead at the scale of an organization, then you need to spend a whole lot of time getting strategy and culture right.

One leader who embodies this approach is the wildly effective Claire Hughes Johnson, chief operating officer of the payments company Stripe. Johnson is so good at what she does that her casual presentations on how to run staff meetings have gone viral. Whenever she onboards a new employee, Johnson leads with the word "empowered" and gets right to the mechanics of absence leadership: "You're going to have a manager. Your manager's important. But they're not with you all day long. What you're doing with your time is your choice, and the impact you have is driven by *your* decisions."[6] Those decisions, we argue in chapters 5 and 6, are guided primarily by strategy and culture. (See the sidebar "Less Control, More Command: Empowerment Leadership in Action.")

It's hard to overstate the emotional power of being unleashed by someone. Most people can remember, even with the watery recall of a distant memory, what it felt like when a teacher or coach or friend made it clear that they saw something better inside us. It's electrifying to be seen not only as we are, rare enough in its own right, but also as the people we might become. When Lisa Skeete Tatum founded Landit, a breakthrough professional development company, she created a space where women and people of color could dwell on their future selves and be valued for their potential. Even a single session with a Landit coach has been described to us as "life-changing."

One female CEO we worked with could summon with spectacular detail a brief exchange with one of her business school professors, who answered a simple clarifying question after class by saying, "Well, when you're a CEO one day . . . " This woman's highest aspiration at the time was to go back to the consulting firm that paid for her degree and get on track to a midlevel advisory role.

It had never occurred to her that she might one day have the audacity to lead a company. In describing the memory to us, now decades old, she could remember the shirt she was wearing that day, how the classroom lighting reflected off the carpeting she was standing on, how her mind canceled out the noise around her for a few seconds as she absorbed the comment. She counts this moment as the beginning of her evolution into someone, in her words, who was "willing to take up real space in the world."

The heady truth is that we all have the ability to release the energy of possibility in someone else's life. For a feel-good illustration of the kind of magic that can happen when you make this choice, consider the runaway success of the show *Queer Eye*. Hosted by a team of five talented lifestyle experts (four identify as gay men, one as gender nonbinary), the show invites viewers into the lives of real-life "hero" protagonists who—with the experts' help—transform their wardrobes, grooming, interior design, eating habits, and often their relationships with work and family.

It all makes for good television, with lots of big reveals and before-and-after moments. But the thing that makes these transformations possible is something that all of us can offer: the unapologetic belief in a better version of someone. By the end of the episode, what's different for each hero is that they *also* believe in that better version of themselves.

Getting out of your own head

Counterintuitively, an "other" orientation can be harder to sustain for people who represent marginalized groups, one of the reasons we love the *Queer Eye* example. The show's hosts often work their magic in spaces where queer identities are rare and sometimes unwelcome, where they have good reason to retreat to a position

Less Control, More Command:
Empowerment Leadership in Action

General Martin Dempsey, former chairman of the Joint Chiefs of Staff, saw the need for precisely this kind of mindset shift in a place you might least expect it: the United States Army.

The army began revisiting its own leadership models in the early 2000s when it started losing ground in the "war on terror"—or, at least, not particularly gaining it. Gone were the days when familiar enemy forces lined up and did things we expected them to do, in the name of national interests that were not so different from our own. Borders had become less relevant on a fast-moving chessboard of globalized risks that could escalate in the time it took to send a text message. The fog of war had gotten foggier.

After a decade of operating in this disorienting reality, the army was ready to talk about what it had learned, and what it wanted to talk about was leadership. In 2012, General Dempsey produced a manifesto on how to lead in this new, less predictable environment.[7] The memo made a passionate case for why a leader's mandate was less about consolidating power and more about prudent decentralization of that power up and down the chain of command.

Dempsey articulated a vision for leadership focused somewhat radically on the performance of subordinates, on creating conditions for other people to increasingly call the shots. In this new framework, leaders would teach their trainees not *what* to think, but *how* to think and make decisions in the murky world of modern warfare, where context and conditions are constantly shifting. He named his philosophy "Mission Command," and, according to Dempsey, nothing less than the army's ability to defend the homeland was on the line.

Dempsey's vision built on the German military concept of *auftragstaktik* and the ideas of a brilliant, nineteenth-century Prussian field marshal remembered as Helmuth von Moltke the Elder. Moltke believed that the only way to prevail in chaotic and uncertain operating environments was to encourage aggressive initiative, autonomy, and ingenuity *at every level*. Everyone, from generals to junior officers, received intensive training in decentralized command, and under Moltke's leadership, the Prussian army delivered a swift, surprise victory in the Franco-Prussian War. Channeling Moltke's prescient vision for an empowered force, Dempsey's doctrine emphasized interpersonal trust, freedom of action, and the need for actors at all levels to be able to think critically and creatively. In this emerging world of faster-mutating and higher-stakes threats, Dempsey insisted that a leader's most important job is to make damn sure that *everyone else* can perform. In short, Dempsey argued, it's no longer all about you, General.

Mission Command offers us not only a new way to lead, but also a new way to *think* about leading. It's a model that challenges leaders to embed trust and strategy into the organization so that they can confidently remove themselves from on-the-ground decisions. It's a mindset focused on how to unleash other people in your presence, so that they can go out and excel in your absence.

We asked decorated former Company Commander Emily Hannenberg how Mission Command was going for the army. In her decade of military service, Hannenberg had distinguished herself spectacularly, including graduation from the Sapper Leader Course,

(*continued*)

a leadership development program that's the grueling combat engineering equivalent of Ranger School. There is healthy debate inside the army over which course is more difficult, and Hannenberg is one of only a hundred or so women in army history to have completed the program successfully.

Hannenberg describes herself and her peers as "all in" on Mission Command, having seen firsthand how it improved unit adaptability and performance. In 2014, she was tapped to train new officers on this new model of leadership as a professor of military science at the Massachusetts Institute of Technology. When Hannenberg talked to us about the payoff of Mission Command, she emphasized heightened access to human potential: "When people are trained and trusted to lead in their own spheres of influence, they find out they can do things they never imagined were possible." In this new model, Hannenberg clarified, her teams weren't waiting for permission to bring the full breadth of their abilities to whatever problem needed solving. They weren't waiting for permission to win.

of self-preservation. Instead, the opposite happens. They show up exposed and emotionally generous, putting everything they've got into unleashing someone else.

Underrepresented leaders sometimes have a harder time looking beyond themselves in a world that still questions, at times, whether who we are may be disqualifying. As two women who check a few unconventional boxes (for example, we're married to each other), we've had our own experiences of costly self-distraction.

A pattern in our own missed opportunities has played out whenever we've chosen to protect ourselves rather than do the exposing work of leadership. One setting that took us years to embrace as inclusive leaders was formal gatherings of colleagues more senior to us. Rather than approach these meetings as opportunities to teach and learn, to lead and be led by peers we respected deeply, too often we entered these spaces with our metaphorical porcupine quills flexed. In our attempt to protect the more vulnerable flesh underneath, we would show up in ways—sometimes too timid, other times too brash—that materially reduced our chance of influence.

That's the irony of many of the tactics we use to protect ourselves as leaders. They can backfire and undermine the perceptions we're working so hard to cultivate. In order to *look* like leaders, we end up behaving like smaller, two-dimensional versions of ourselves. We obscure the parts of ourselves that real leadership demands, cutting off access to our full humanity. In the choice to insulate ourselves from the judgment of others, we disconnect from leadership's core mandate to make those very same people better.

We've spent too much of our own careers caring what other people think of us, of our identities as gay women, of the strength of Frances's opinions or the way Anne's voice sometimes shakes when she feels strongly about something. First of all, to be clear, while some people have occasionally held those things against us, most people didn't notice, didn't care, or actually preferred interacting with the raw, unvarnished versions of us. More important, if our ambition was to lead, then we were asking the wrong question. The relevant question wasn't "What do these people think of me?"; it was "What can I do to help make these people better?" That's the shift that empowerment leadership demands.

We're not suggesting that you disappear behind others and give up your pursuit of status and recognition. But we *are* creating

Wait, Can't It Sometimes Be about Me?

The short answer to that question is "of course." Leadership is about unleashing other people, but it doesn't mean that your own recovery and improvement aren't things that need regular attention. A focus on yourself may be necessary for any number of good reasons, including your own sanity. To be "on" from a leadership standpoint—to channel the empathy, commitment, and presence to successfully enable other people—can require a level of energy that's only sustainable with regular time-outs from the leadership path. Getting better can also mean investing in the skills you need to gain a new leadership platform or to earn the trust of people around you. As we will explore in our next chapter, other people's willingness to be led by you requires at least some conviction that you know what you're doing. That might require you to develop new skills.

Case in point: one health-care entrepreneur we worked with joined a local improv troupe to remind himself what it felt like to simply play as an adult. A passionate company builder and father of three, "Jason" (we promised to protect his identity) craved an alternative space outside the office to flex creative muscles he wasn't using in his daily life. At this point in his company's life cycle, Jason was doing lots of operational firefighting, which was less energizing to him than the work he had done in the company's earlier, innovation-focused stage. Performing improv was fun for Jason and also helped

a distinction between that game and the practice of leadership, in a world that often conflates the two. If you seek to lead, then your focus—by definition—shifts from elevating yourself to protecting, developing, and enabling the people around you. It's him communicate more effectively. The experience made him more present with his team and more empathetic as a listener. It was the ultimate after-hours activity, highly restorative while also improving his ability to do his day job.

Improv made Jason more effective as a leader, but he wasn't leading while up on stage, "yes, and . . ."-ing his fellow performers.* This is a simple but important distinction, which can sometimes get blurred in a work culture that has normalized Ping-Pong as a legitimate, on-the-clock activity. Jason was growing as a professional and recovering as a human being, but he wasn't having impact as a leader until he got down off the stage and returned to the challenge of empowering *other* people.

In our experience, it's generally one or the other. You can improve yourself or the people around you, but it's difficult to do both at the same time. We advise being intentional about this distinction and doing the work on you away from the office. Yes, take that vacation (please!) and after-hours management course. Hit the Appalachian Trail and read a great leadership book.** Then get back to the business of leading whenever you come back to work again.

---

* "Yes, and . . . " is a core improv principle that challenges you to accept reality as it is offered to you and then build on that reality to develop a compelling scene.

** Definitely do this.

---

the unapologetic part of this. Think conductor or director rather than star of the show. Your job is to make Oscar-worthy movies about *other people*. (See the sidebar "Wait, Can't It Sometimes Be about Me?")

Getting started: How about now?

Once you've made the leadership pivot, your job is to see the full humanity of the people you seek to lead, including their ability to evolve. Only when you can imagine a better version of someone can you play a role in helping to unleash them. If you don't have confidence in someone's growth potential, then you can do many things with that person, but leading isn't one of them. You can oversee, supervise, govern, persuade, and endure them. You can get through the day and instruct them to do things. We don't recommend this approach, but you can certainly do it, and it arguably describes a lot of what happens in today's default employer-employee dynamic.

Leadership is predicated on the idea that human beings can adapt and that we can play an important role in each other's adaptation. This progression, in turn, requires a leader's willingness to both believe in someone else's unrealized potential and find ways to communicate that conviction. In other words, it requires that you not keep this beautiful insight to yourself.

There are countless ways to tell someone what you see in them, and we recommend experimenting with signals that feel authentic to you. For example, spotlight their work in a meeting, or ask them for advice before they've "earned" the right to give it, or offer them your full, device-free attention, a strikingly powerful gesture in this pandemic of digital distraction that we're all living through right now. A particularly powerful sign of your conviction is to give someone the ball again after they've just missed the proverbial shot. Believing in someone sometimes means giving them space to stumble and learn along the way.

We also advise you to be direct. Sit someone down and tell them about the strengths you've observed, being as sincere and specific as you can in your descriptions. Use dates, times, and details, illustrating the positive impacts of their behavior on you and others.

We will talk more about how to give effective feedback later in the book, but this is more radical counsel than it sounds. Most organizational cultures rely on negative prompts for improvement, which are far less effective than positive reinforcement.

To help people practice this leadership skill, one of our favorite exercises is to send them out into the world as ambassadors of other people's awesomeness (OPA).[c] It works like this: choose someone in whom you see some kind of talent, however big or small, and find a genuine way to let them know that you've noticed. You see what they're capable of today and—this is for leadership bonus points— you see where that gift might take them tomorrow if they decide to share it more often. Start with a person close to you and work outward from there.

The goal here is to start getting in the habit of an external leadership orientation, away from the magnetic pull of our own thoughts and experiences and toward the potential of the people we seek to lead. While you're at it, go ahead and generate some unexpected joy. Talk to different kinds of people, from loved ones to colleagues to strangers you happen to catch in the act of expressing their gifts. Include people who are like you and people who are not, both demographically and from the standpoint of worldview and personality.

Be sure to include at least one person who is convinced that they are past their alleged prime, someone who believes they peaked years or even decades ago. As you'll discover out on the OPA trail, people don't stop reacting powerfully to being seen once they reach full adulthood and its corresponding delusion that they've stopped evolving as people. Indeed, in our experience, it can be even more impactful for seasoned professionals to be reminded of their capacity for unrestrained growth.

c. To our international readers: We are aware of our flagrant abuse of the words "super" and "awesome." We invite you to replace these words with your preferred terms at any point in the book.

The unapologetic leader

An extraordinary amount of energy is being stored up in the distance between who we are and who we might become. In 2017, Gallup did a survey of the American workplace that found that close to 70 percent of employees are not engaged at work.[8] Pause and take that number in, even its directional implications. This means that most of us are walking around with mostly unused capacity most of the time, and it is nothing less than an astonishing opportunity cost. Leadership that's not about you gives people license to engage more fully with the organizations around them. It unleashes people to achieve things they never dreamed were possible. On the other side of that kind of leadership is a remade world.

This revolution will require us to change the way we think about leadership. Paul Revere earned glory by tearing through the Massachusetts countryside, but the real plot point in leadership history is what happened next, the men and women who stepped out into the streets of Lexington and Concord to determine their own destinies.[d] We believe you can trace a line from their courage to the hundreds of civil rights marchers in Selma, Alabama, to the thousands who lined up behind Gandhi and marched for self-rule, to the millions of global supporters of movements like #MeToo and Black Lives Matter and their assertions of a universal right to dignity, regardless of who you are.

What will be the focus of your own leadership story? Will it be about the power you stockpiled and protected? Or about how much more you achieved by using that power to unleash the people around you? This book is about choosing the second path, unapologetically. It's about what leaders say and do and feel when they're at

---

d. Anne was not the first cross-dressed minuteman. Prudence Cummings Wright famously fought in the battle of Lexington and Concord, leading a small armed militia of self-described "minutewomen" disguised as men.

their most effective. It's about leadership as an adventure of infinite possibility, one that starts by honoring the true (and ancient) art of empowering everyone around you. Once you make that shift in perspective, then the next set of questions is about the practical ways to pull it all off. We begin that conversation in chapter 2, the first ring of our leadership framework. Empowerment begins, we believe, with trust.

GUT CHECK

Questions for Reflection

- ✓ Why are you reading this book? Why is it worth your time and energy to get better at the practice of leadership?

- ✓ How does the performance of other people change when you're around? If you observe any patterns, write them down.

- ✓ In your capacity as a leader, how much of your time do you spend thinking about yourself and your own needs versus other people and *their* needs?

- ✓ When do you reliably empower other people? When has that investment in others been easy for you? When has it been hard?

- ✓ When you succeed in unleashing other people, what is different about your "state"? How does your energy and ability to focus change?

PART ONE

PRESENCE

The practical frame on leadership we use in this book is that it's all about empowering other people, in both our presence and our absence. In this first section—what we call "presence" chapters—we focus on opportunities for leadership when you're in the proverbial room, when the people you seek to lead are within your immediate reach (a text message counts, too). This is what we mean by "presence."

In chapter 2, we explore how to build and maintain a foundation of trust, the starting point for empowerment leadership. In chapter 3, we lay out a battle-tested framework for creating conditions in which other people can reliably excel. We examine our very rational, human tendency to sometimes dilute our commitment to the success of other people or lower our standards for the people we're most devoted to. Finally, we discuss how to unapologetically defy these instincts and make sure everyone around us can thrive.

We also make the case for truly inclusive leadership, for enabling people who don't look and think and talk like you. In chapter 4, we discuss how to build diverse teams that excel, not just in spite of their differences, but precisely because of them. We give you a framework for understanding the escalating noise around the topic of diversity and use our experience with large-scale, transformational inclusion initiatives to show how effective leadership can create the conditions for more and varied people to thrive—and for organizations to benefit wildly from it.

In effect, this section is about mastering the inner rings of our empowerment leadership model: *trust*, *love*, and *belonging*. Again, when you get it right, your presence as a leader has progressively positive impact, starting with yourself and then expanding to more and more people.

Let's begin.

2

TRUST

On a Friday afternoon in the spring of 2017, Travis Kalanick, then CEO of Uber, walked into a conference room at the company's minimalist Bay Area headquarters. A wildly talented deputy, Meghan Joyce, general manager for the United States and Canada, had orchestrated the meeting. Joyce was convinced that we could be helpful, but that was not our starting point. From everything we'd read about the iconic, ride-hailing startup, it looked like a company with little hope of redemption.[a]

First, some context: Uber had disrupted at least one industry, but its astonishing success seemed to come at the price of basic decency. A #deleteUber campaign began shortly after the company appeared to take advantage of a taxi strike in response to President Trump's travel ban. A few months later, Uber engineer Susan Fowler blogged about her experience of harassment and discrimination in a culture she convincingly portrayed as ruthless.[1] Footage then emerged of Kalanick interacting with an Uber driver, where he

a. At the authors' discretion, some details have been changed to maintain voice and make storytelling less cumbersome. In particular, despite our standard use of "we," the authors were not physically together at all times.

appeared dismissive of the difficulties of earning a living in a post-Uber world. Other charges leveled at the company in this period reinforced Uber's reputation as a cold-blooded operator that would do almost anything to win.

It did not help the company's position that some of its challenges had morphed into public reckonings with ills that plagued the rest of the tech sector, too.[2] These included inertia and confusion when it came to building safe and healthy workplaces. Companies that had no problem achieving the impossible commercially seemed overwhelmed by how to create conditions in which a large, diverse workforce could thrive.

As Frances waited for Kalanick to make his entrance, she braced herself for the smug CEO she had read about. That person wasn't the one who walked in. Kalanick arrived humbled and introspective. He had thought a lot about how some of the cultural values he'd instilled in the company—the very values that had fueled Uber's success—had also been misused and distorted on his watch. He revealed deep respect for what his team had achieved, but he also recognized that some of the people he had placed in leadership roles lacked the training, mentorship, or breathing room to be effective.

Whatever mistakes Kalanick had made up to this point, here was a leader trying to do the right thing. He and Frances took fast turns at a whiteboard, sketching out possibilities for the company. By the time Arianna Huffington, the sole woman on Uber's board at the time, came in to offer her perspective, Frances was open to the idea that we could be useful. Huffington was just coming from a heated session with female employees, and you could tell she had absorbed a lot of pain. The scene was the opposite of what we had come to expect from hands-off, Silicon Valley boards. Huffington was in the trenches with Kalanick, and her sleeves-up commitment moved us.

Retreating back to our home in Cambridge, Massachusetts, we debated whether to take on the project. There were lots of reasons to stay away from it. The work would be hard and its outcome uncertain, to say nothing of the brutal commute. There were real problems to solve, including a frustrated workforce and a brand heading toward toxic. But we realized that if we could do it here, if we could help get Uber back on the right path, then we could give license to countless others to restore humanity to organizations that had lost their way.

So where did we begin? We started with trust.[3]

The foundation of leadership

We think about trust as rare and precious, and yet it's the basis for almost everything we do as civilized people. Trust is the reason we're willing to exchange our hard-earned paychecks for goods and services, pledge our lives to another person in marriage, cast a ballot for someone who will represent our interests. We rely on laws and contracts as safety nets, but even those systems are ultimately built on trust in the institutions that enforce them. We don't *know* that justice will be served if something goes wrong, but we have enough faith in the system to make deals with relative strangers. It's not coincidental that trust ultimately found its way into the official US motto, "In God We Trust." Even if trust in our earthly structures erodes, it's so vital to the national project that we threw in a higher-order backstop.

As we previewed in chapter 1, trust is also the input that makes the leadership equation work. If leadership is about empowering others, in your presence and your absence, then trust is the emotional framework that allows that service to be freely exchanged. I'm willing to be led by you because I trust you. I'm willing to give up some of my cherished autonomy and put my well-being in your hands because I trust you. In turn, you're willing to rely on me because you trust me. You trust that I will make decisions that advance our shared mission, even when you're not in the room. The more trust that accumulates between us, the better this works.

How do you build up stores of this essential leadership capital? Here's the basic formula: people tend to trust you when they think they are interacting with the real you (authenticity), when they have faith in your judgment and competence (logic), and when they believe that you care about them (empathy). When trust is lost, it can almost always be traced back to a breakdown in one of these three drivers. You can find the roots of this framework in Aristotle's writing on the elements of effective persuasion, where he argued that you need to ground your case in logos, pathos, and ethos. You will also find this pattern in much of modern psychology literature. (See figure 2-1.)

FIGURE 2-1

The trust triangle

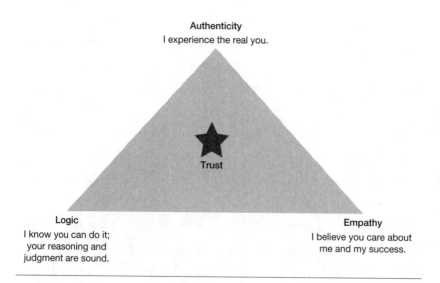

Authenticity
I experience the real you.

Trust

Logic
I know you can do it;
your reasoning and
judgment are sound.

Empathy
I believe you care about
me and my success.

Should we trust you?

What signals are you sending about whether the world should trust you? We don't always realize what information (or more often, misinformation) we're putting out there about our own trustworthiness. What's worse, stress tends to amplify the problem. Under pressure, we often double down on behaviors that undermine trust. For example, we unconsciously mask our true selves in a job interview, even though it's precisely the type of less than fully authentic behavior that's going to reduce our chance of being hired.

The good news is that most of us generate a stable pattern of trust signals, which means a small change in behavior can go a long way. First, we tend to get in our own way, in the same way, over and over again. In moments when trust is broken (or fails to get any real traction), it's usually the same driver—authenticity, empathy, or logic—that gets wobbly on us. In fact, we call this pattern of setbacks your trust "wobble." Your wobble is the driver that's most likely to get shaky in periods of low trust. Everyone, it turns out, has a wobble.

We also all have a driver where we're rock solid, one that stays strong and steady in our interactions with others, regardless of the circumstances. One of the three trust drivers rarely lets us down, even if we're woken up out of a dead sleep at 3:00 a.m. and asked to perform. We call this pattern your trust "anchor." Your anchor is the attribute that's *least* likely to get wobbly on you, even when the proverbial clouds start to gather and winds start to howl.

Your own trust diagnosis

Before getting started, we suggest identifying a compelling reason to do this work. If you could build more trust tomorrow than you did today, how would that impact your effectiveness as a leader? As usual, we suggest writing down the thoughts that come to mind.

Now think of a recent moment when you were not trusted as much as you wanted to be. Maybe you lost an important sale or didn't get that stretch assignment. Maybe someone doubted your ability to execute or simply kept their distance from you on a project. Here's the hard part: give this other person in the story—let's call them your skeptic—the benefit of the doubt. Assume that their reservations were valid, and you were the one responsible for the breakdown in trust. This exercise only works if you own it.

If you had to choose from the short list of trust attributes, which of the three got in your way? From the skeptic's perspective, which got wobbly on you? Did they think you might be putting your own interests first? Did the interaction feel all about you? That's an *empathy* block. Did they question the rigor of your analysis or your ability to execute on an ambitious plan? That's a *logic* problem. Or did they think you might be misrepresenting some part of your story, exaggerating the upside or downplaying the risks? That's an *authenticity* issue.

Whichever it was, that's your wobble, at least in this interaction. Draw a trust triangle and put a squiggly line under the unsteady attribute. If your wobble was empathy, for example, then your trust triangle would look like the one in figure 2-2.

Assuming your skeptic didn't flee the room or laugh at the absurdity of your plan, something was also going right for you on the trust front. Which of the three trust pillars was unwavering? That's your anchor in this story. Go back to your triangle and put a plus sign next to your anchor. If you chose logic as your anchor, for example, then your triangle should now look like the one in figure 2-3.

FIGURE 2-2

Which is your trust "wobble"?

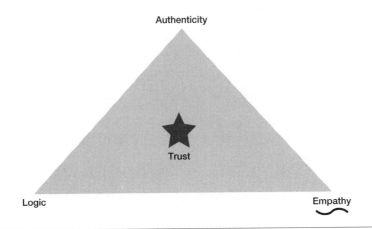

FIGURE 2-3

Which is your trust "anchor"?

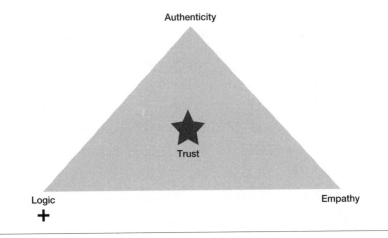

Test your hypothesis

Our advice is to bring at least one other person along for your diagnostic ride. Sharing your analysis can be clarifying—even liberating—and will help you test and refine your hypothesis. Ideally, pick a thought partner who knows you well. About 20 percent of self-assessors need a round of revision, so choose a partner who can keep you honest if your analysis is off. Exchanging wobble stories with another person can also mediate any shame you may associate with losing trust. Wobbling is a universal human experience. What matters to your leadership mandate is what you choose to do about it.

For the advanced trust builders out there, consider going back and testing your analysis directly with your skeptic. This conversation alone can be an enormously powerful way to build and rebuild trust. Taking responsibility for a wobble reveals your humanity (authenticity) and analytic chops (logic), while communicating your commitment to the relationship (empathy).

Your challenge now is to look at your pattern of wobbles and anchors across *multiple* examples. Pick the top three or four interactions that stand out to you, for whatever reason, and do a quick trust diagnostic for each one. What do your *typical* wobbles and anchors seem to be? Does the pattern change under stress or with different kinds of stakeholders? For example, do you wobble in one way with your direct reports, but in a different way with people who have authority over you (this isn't uncommon)?

Over the last decade, we've helped all kinds of leaders wrestle with trust issues, from seasoned politicians to millennial entrepreneurs to leaders of disruptive, multibillion-dollar companies (including Uber, which we'll return to at the end of this chapter). When one retail CEO we advised identified his wobble, we watched him fix it in his next interaction. His challenge was empathy, and small changes in behavior—things like making eye contact, asking better questions, putting away his phone—had an immediate impact on his relationship with his team. In the next section, we offer some effective strategies for overcoming your own trust wobble, starting with the most common wobble we encounter among high-achieving leaders: empathy.

Empathy: Looking out for number one

Your wobble may be empathy if people often think you care more about yourself than about others. As we explored in chapter 1, this kind of signaling is a major barrier to empowerment leadership. If people think you're primarily in it for you, then they're far less willing to be led by you.

Empathy wobbles are common among people who are analytical and driven to learn. For many empathy wobblers, boredom is an enemy that must be taken down at all costs, in whatever corners of our daily lives it may be lurking. Long lines and slow traffic. Predictable TV storylines.[b] Meetings with colleagues who may need longer than we do to "get it."

The tools and experience of modern leadership also make it increasingly difficult to communicate empathy, with twenty-four-hour demands on our time and multiple devices competing for our attention at any given moment. We also tend to have less time for recovery, which leads us to seek moments of micro-recovery throughout our day, sometimes smack in the middle of conversations with the very people we're working to empower and lead.

b. One of us only watches television with a remote control at the ready, which she uses to "speed up" scenes that she thinks will be boring, inevitably missing much of the plot. One of us, the one who happens to have the keyboard right now, is made crazy by this behavior.

And all those open-office plans—now widely embraced for their practicality and design value—aren't necessarily helping. There can sometimes be nowhere to pause and catch your breath in a truly communal workspace.[4]

We advise empathy wobblers to pay close attention to their behavior in group settings, particularly when other people have the floor. Consider the standard meeting example: an empathy wobbler's engagement tends to be sky high at the kickoff of a meeting (you might learn something!) until the moment they understand the concepts and contribute their ideas. At this point, their engagement plummets and remains low until the gathering mercifully comes to an end. We call this dramatic arc the "agony of the super smart" (or ASS).

How do you signal you understand something before everyone else? Ah, well, the possibilities are endless. You could flamboyantly multitask, or find ways to look bored, or look down at your phone the first chance you get. Anything to make it clear that this meeting is beneath you. Unfortunately, the cost of these indulgences is trust. If you signal that you matter more than everyone else, then you can do many things, but being trusted as a leader isn't one of them.

The prescription is easy to describe, but harder to execute: change your objective from getting what *you* need in the meeting to making sure everyone else gets what *they* need. In other words, take radical responsibility for everyone else in the room. Share the burden of moving the dialogue forward, even if it's not your meeting. Search for the resonant examples that will bring the concepts to life, and don't disengage until everyone in the room understands. Note that this is almost impossible to do as long as texting or checking email is an option, so put away your devices (everyone knows you're not taking notes on their good ideas). See the graphic representation of this pivot in figure 2-4.[5]

The headline here is that the antidote to an empathy wobble is presence. What do the people around you need from you as a

FIGURE 2-4

New meeting rules for empathy wobblers

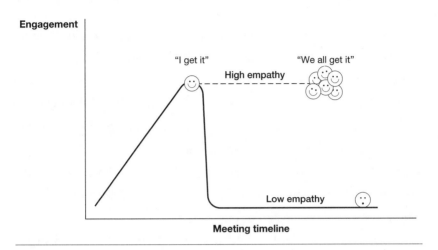

leader? What else could you be doing in this moment to empower them? It's impossible to find out if your head is somewhere else, on your own needs and ambitions (and devices). The last thing we'll say is this: if you do nothing else, put down your phone. You'll be amazed at the immediate uptick in trust—and you may even get to end those meetings sooner. We've seen organizations that adopt high-empathy meeting norms cut the time they spend in meetings *in half*. (See the sidebar "Empathy and the Future of Work.")

Logic: Large but not quite in charge

Your wobble may be logic if people don't always have confidence in the rigor of your ideas—or full faith in your ability to deliver on them. The good news is the problem is typically rooted in the *perception* of wobbly logic rather than the reality of it. Either

Empathy and the Future of Work

It has not been a banner decade for trust in the American workplace. We've grown increasingly skeptical that our employers will tell us the truth, have our backs in hard times, or compensate us fairly for the work we do. As massive forces such as globalization and technological innovation continue to reshape our experience of work, we're pretty sure that someone else—or some*thing* else—will be doing our jobs in the future. We're increasingly willing to believe, with good reason, that the game is rigged for an elite shareholder class that rarely has to follow the same rules we do.

If we look at this pattern through a trust lens, we would argue the US economy is dealing with a big, bad empathy wobble. Americans have become convinced that a growing number of companies are in it solely to enrich themselves, not to be of service to their customers (or, heaven forbid, their employees). This belief gets reinforced by everything from less-than-living wages to draconian noncompete agreements to the willful mishandling of our personal data.

Organizations that persuade us otherwise have a massive advantage. Iconic outdoor clothing retailer Patagonia has consistently prioritized social impact over financial returns, serving as a model for "not about you" leadership from its earliest days. Patagonia founder Yvon Chouinard says he set out to build a company whose primary mission was to take care of customers, employees, and the planet.[6] Patagonia now generates about $1 billion in sales each year, and has donated 1 percent of all revenue back to environmental nonprofits since 1985.

As trust in corporate America has eroded, Patagonia CEO Rose Marcario has doubled down on the company's commitment to serve something bigger than its own success—and, in doing so, has quadrupled revenue during her tenure.[7] She reinforces the company's values by closing stores and offices so Patagonia employees can do more important things than sell clothes, like vote on election day. She also very visibly sued the US government in 2017 for misuse of public lands.[8] To remove any doubt regarding Patagonia's raison d'être, Marcario even changed the company's mission statement from "Do no unnecessary harm" to "We're in business to save our home planet."[9]

We spoke with Marcela Escobari, who now leads the Workforce of the Future Initiative at the Brookings Institute, about how to rebuild trust at the scale of an economy. "Do we all need to Be Like Rose?" we asked. "Yes and no" was her answer. Before shifting her focus to the evolution of work, Escobari led USAID's efforts to address issues of poverty, inequality, and citizen security in Latin America. She witnessed firsthand how trust was being destroyed in places like Venezuela—and also how it was being built and rebuilt in countries like Peru. In a world where mistrust is on the rise, her advice to business leaders is, yes, take the long view and make it about something more than your shareholders—channel your inner Rose Marcario— but also "never forget that investing in people has the possibility of infinite returns."

Escobari argues that a higher-skilled and more resilient workforce may be the fastest path to a future where we trust each other again. Although there's an obvious role for the public sector in driving this change, Escobari knows that the private sector is indispensable and is energized by a renewed corporate focus on retraining employees

(continued)

(rather than laying them off) as technology transforms the workplace. She cites many examples of companies effectively preparing their employees for a future of work that is not so far away, including companies like Costco, JetBlue, and Trader Joe's. We've even seen companies at the scale of Walmart begin to invest in employee education in innovative ways. In 2018, Walmart made headlines with its "dollar-a-day" education benefit that gives associates the chance to earn a college degree through nonprofit partner universities, paying the equivalent of $1 a day as they progress toward a bachelor's or associate's degree.[10]

Our education bias is clear—see our histories and career choices—but we believe a big part of the remedy to America's trust wobble is to increase fair access to opportunities to develop a competitive skill set. We need to level our winners-take-all playing field in a number of ways, starting with the chance to thrive in the workplace of the future. In this country's founding documents, we promised to defend each other's pursuit of happiness—not happiness itself, but the pursuit of it—as a sacred, inalienable right. Until we treat that promise with reverence again, we're not going to solve our collective trust problem.

As one of our heroes, Brazilian thinker and teacher Paulo Freire, said, "What the educator does is make it possible for students to become themselves."[11] There is no higher human need than to realize our full potential, and no greater act of empathy than to enable that evolution in others. We believe the future of work—and of the planet Marcario has vowed to save—depends on our willingness to exchange the gift of each other's transformation.

way, the effect is the same: if we're not sure your judgment can handle the road ahead, then we're less likely to want you at the wheel.

In the rare cases when wobbly logic is truly the problem, we advise going back to the data. Root the case you're making in evidence, speak to the things you know to be true, and then (and this is the hard part) *stop there*. One reason Larry Bird was such an extraordinary basketball player was that he only took shots he knew he could reliably make. That choice made him different from so many other players, who often let ego and adrenaline cloud their shooting judgment. Bird studied and practiced so relentlessly that by the time the ball left his hands in the heat of competition, he knew exactly where it was going. If logic is your wobble, take Bird's example and learn to "play within yourself."

Once you get comfortable with how that feels, start expanding what you know. Along the way, don't hesitate to learn from what *other people* know. Other people's insights are among the most valuable—and overlooked—resources in the workplace, but accessing them requires a willingness to reveal you don't have all the answers, something leaders often resist. We learned this lesson the hard way early in our careers, too often preferring to hide out and polish our own flawed logic rather than be vulnerable and ask for help. This choice cost us not only the opportunity to improve at a faster pace, but also the chance to build stronger relationships with our colleagues (asking for help can also reveal what energizes you professionally).

For most logic wobblers, however, rigor isn't the issue. A more likely explanation for the breakdown in trust is that you're not communicating your ideas effectively. There are generally two ways to communicate complex thoughts. The first way takes your audience on a journey, with twists and turns and context and dramatic tension, until they eventually get the payoff. Many of the world's best storytellers use this technique. You can visualize this approach as an inverted triangle with an enchantingly circuitous route to the point. If logic is your wobble, however, this is a risky path. Without enough confidence in your narrative destination, the audience is tempted to abandon you along the way.

Try flipping the triangle. Start with your headline and then offer reinforcing evidence to back it up. This shift signals clarity of vision and full command of the facts. Everyone has a much better chance of following your logic, and even if you get interrupted along the way, you've at least had a chance to communicate your key idea. See figure 2-5 for an illustration of this pivot.

Flipping the triangle can immediately steady a logic wobble and reduce the likelihood of other workplace injustices, such as having your idea "stolen" in a meeting, just minutes after you've shared it. More often than not, our sticky-fingered colleagues are simply flipping the triangle *for* us.

FIGURE 2-5

Communication for logic wobblers

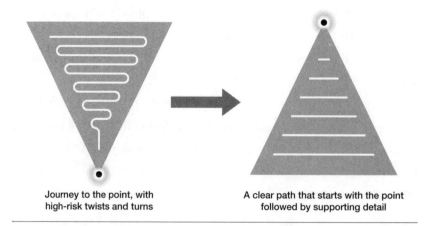

Journey to the point, with
high-risk twists and turns

A clear path that starts with the point
followed by supporting detail

Authenticity: Who was that masked man?

You may have an authenticity wobble if people feel they're not getting access to the "real" you, to a full and complete accounting of what you know, think, and feel. If the version of reality you present feels overly curated or strategic, an invisible wall can form between you and the people around you.

A quick test: How different is your professional persona from the one that shows up around family and friends? If there's a real difference, what are you getting in return for masking or minimizing certain parts of yourself? What's the payoff (for example, approval or a sense of safety)? If you can easily answer these questions, then authenticity may be on your short list of challenges.

To be our "real selves" sounds nice in theory, but there can be powerful, hard-earned incentives to hold back certain truths. The calculation can be highly practical at times, if wrenching, as in the decision to stay closeted in a workplace that's hostile to queer identities. There may also be times when expressing your authentic feelings may be ill-advised: women are disproportionately penalized for negative emotions in the workplace, and black men remain burdened by the false stereotype that they are predisposed to anger.[12]

We're not talking about moments of prudent self-censorship, which sometimes can't be divorced from a larger context of bias or low psychological safety.[13] Instead, we're talking about inauthenticity as a *strategy* for navigating the workplace. While this approach may help you solve short-term problems, it puts an artificial cap on trust and, by extension, your ability to lead. If we sense you're withholding the truth or concealing your authentic self, if we don't know what your genuine beliefs and values are, then we're far less willing to make ourselves vulnerable to you in the ways that leadership demands.

Although this pattern can present in different ways, we've observed its cost up close in the performance of diverse teams. Diversity can be a tremendous asset in today's marketplace, and the companies that get it right often build up powerful competitive headwinds. But, in our experience, this advantage isn't automatic. Simply populating your team with diverse perspectives and experiences doesn't always translate into better performance.[14]

In fact, the uncomfortable truth is that diverse teams can *underperform* homogenous teams if they're not managed actively for differences among team members, due in part to a phenomenon called the *common information effect*.[15] It works like this: As human beings, we tend to focus on the things we have in common with other people. We tend to seek out and affirm our shared knowledge, as it confirms our value and kinship with the group. In diverse teams, by definition, this limits the amount of information that's readily available for collective decision making.

In figure 2-6, we illustrate this dynamic for two teams of three people, one team where the three teammates are different from each other and another where they're similar. When difference is unmanaged, the common information effect gives the homogenous teams a natural advantage.

FIGURE 2-6

Available information for diverse and homogeneous teams

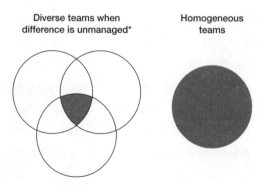

Diverse teams when
difference is unmanaged*

Homogeneous
teams

* The common information effect focuses a team on shared knowledge and limits access to unique information.

In other words, if both diverse and homogenous teams are managed in exactly the same way—if they simply follow the same best practices in group facilitation, for example—the homogenous team is likely to perform better. No amount of feedback or number of trust falls can overcome the strength of the common information effect.

But here's the thing: the common information effect only holds when we're willing to wobble on authenticity. When we choose to bring our unique selves to the table, the parts of ourselves that are actually different from other people, then diversity can create an unbeatable advantage by *expanding* the amount of information the team can access. Indeed, the world starts to look a lot more like figure 2-7, where an inclusive three-person team is likely to outperform (read truly dominate) the other two teams.

This expansion relies on the courage of authenticity wobblers. Believe us when we say we know this is hard—and sometimes too much to ask. At every step of our careers, we've been tempted to dilute who we are in the world. Although we're as white as they come, we're two queer women with strong opinions and high ambition, for ourselves and other people. One of us is most comfortable in men's clothing and shoes that ask for nothing in return. In certain contexts, these things make us different.

FIGURE 2-7

Available information for inclusive teams

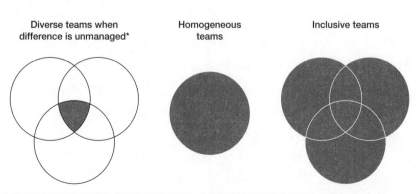

| Diverse teams when difference is unmanaged* | Homogeneous teams | Inclusive teams |

* The common information effect focuses a team on shared knowledge and limits access to unique information.

But if those of us who are different give in to the pressure to hold back our unique selves, then we suppress the most valuable parts of ourselves. Not only do we end up concealing the very thing the world needs most from us—our differences—but we also make it harder for people to trust us in leadership, continuing a flywheel of diminishment that keeps the status quo firmly in place. The smaller we choose to make ourselves, the less likely we are to take up the space required to lead.

Here's the reason to care, even if you don't identify as different: all of us pay the price of inauthentic interactions, and all of us have a better chance of thriving in inclusive environments where authenticity can flourish. Which means that gender bias is not just a woman's problem. Systemic racism is not just an African-American or Latinx problem. It's our shared moral and organizational imperative to create workplaces where the burdens of being different are shouldered by all of us.

We will talk a lot more about how to do this in chapter 4, but the punch line is that it's not as hard as it may seem. Inclusion is an urgent, achievable goal that requires far less audacity than disrupting industries or growing complex organizations, things organizations do every day without fear and confusion shutting down progress. If we all take full responsibility for leading companies where diversity can thrive, and we all take full responsibility for showing up in them authentically, then our chances of building trust—and achieving true inclusion—start to look pretty good.

So wear whatever makes you feel fabulous. Pay less attention to what you think people want to hear and more attention to what you need to say to them. Reveal your full humanity to the world, regardless of what your critics say. And while you're at it, take exquisite care of people who are different from you with confidence that their difference is the very thing that could unleash you. (See the sidebar "Risking Authenticity in the Digital Age.")

Getting back to Uber

What was Uber's wobble? Uber was certainly wobbling when we arrived, and we're on record for calling it "a hot mess" at the time.[16] Let's revisit the basic trust-related facts: on the *empathy* front, the company had improved the lives of an unthinkable number of consumers, but many of the concerns of key stakeholders remained unaddressed, including employees demanding a healthy workplace and drivers looking for more support in their pursuit of a decent living.[17] When it came to *logic*, despite Uber's trajectory of hypergrowth, there were still open questions about the long-term viability of the company's business model.[18] Although some of these questions were reasonable to ask any company at this stage, it was time to start answering them. It was also time to ensure that Uber's management ranks had the skills to lead an organization of its expansive scale and scope.[19] Finally, at the heart of its *authenticity* challenges, no one was completely sure they were getting the full story.[20]

Kalanick knew Uber had a trust problem.[21] By the time he invited Frances to join the company as Uber's first senior vice president for strategy and leadership, a number of initiatives were already underway to steady the company's biggest wobbles. In response to learning about Fowler's experience through her blog post, Kalanick brought in former US Attorney General Eric Holder to lead an internal investigation on harassment and discrimination, and work had begun to implement Holder's sweeping recommendations.[22] In addition, new driver-tipping functionality was about to be rolled out, which would go on to generate $600 million in additional driver compensation in the first year of its launch.[23] New safety features were also in development to give drivers and riders new tools to protect themselves.[24]

Kalanick did not get the chance to see most of his trust-building initiatives to completion, at least not from the chief executive's chair. In June of 2017, the board removed him as CEO while he was

Risking Authenticity in the Digital Age

Authenticity in leadership can be particularly hard when it feels as if everyone's watching, an awareness that's heightened by social media and an unforgiving internet. The response to putting yourself out there—to say nothing of making the inevitable missteps—can be swift and harsh. This environment creates a powerful incentive to wobble on authenticity and conceal the honest, vulnerable parts of ourselves.

We believe the cost of giving in—and hiding out—is too high. Without authenticity, you won't be fully trusted. And without being fully trusted, you won't be able to build a leadership platform that's worthy of you and your potential for impact. Here's our best advice for how to reveal who you are in an age when everyone's a critic.

Take back control from your primate brain. The part of your brain that's wired for survival does an excellent job of protecting you, but it shouldn't always be calling the shots. For one thing, it's highly unreliable at evaluating threats (no, your upcoming speech is not going to kill you, despite the high levels of adrenaline being pumped into your system). Your primate brain is also not playing the long game. It was designed to get you to the end of the day, not to the end of a leadership journey filled with meaning and impact. Buddhism has been wrestling with how to master this part of the mind for thousands of years, and the modern mindfulness movement has created a bridge to accessible tools and practices that can be enormously helpful. Our advice is to at least give them a fair look.[25]

Find your authenticity triggers. Figure out the people and things that tend to pull your full humanity to the surface. Is it your beloved spouse? Favorite sports team? Passion for Harry

Potter trivia? Surround yourself with reminders of these things
or—better yet—find ways to somehow bring them with you
into spaces where an inauthentic version of you has a habit of
showing up. In the not-so-distant past, Anne sometimes struggled with authenticity when pitching new investors, a scenario
that often felt safer behind a two-dimensional mask. One thing
that made a difference was to incorporate stories about our son
into those conversations, as his experience inspired the company she was launching. This choice made it easier for Anne
to show up as herself and be an effective messenger of the
company's vision.

Drop the script. Make sure you're not emphasizing logic at the
cost of authenticity. There is an obvious upside to leaders being
informed and articulate, but when it comes to trust, we also crave
access to the person behind the talking points. Find moments
to keep it real with people and communicate your unscripted
thoughts and ideas. Start with low-risk settings, if needed, such
as intimate lunches or meetings with allies. Dial up the stakes
as you get increasingly comfortable flexing your authenticity
muscles.

Give us the "why." What drives you to do what you do every
day? What has called you to the practice of leadership? Many
leaders keep these fundamental truths to themselves, sometimes
simply out of habit, missing an opportunity to build trust by
revealing what matters most to them. If you don't answer these
questions for your colleagues, then they'll have no choice but to
fill in the blanks themselves, right or wrong.

(continued)

Learn in public. At some point, it became a false badge of honor to think something and never waiver from that thought. Give yourself the freedom to update your point of view based on new information or experiences. Do it out in the open and model what it looks like to have the courage to evolve. Not only will we get to experience a more authentic version of you—the human brain is constantly updating and refreshing—but you will also give the rest of us permission to learn and keep an open mind. A great thing about authenticity is that it's crazy infectious.

Build a team. Authenticity is not a solo sport. It should not be attempted alone in the private distortion chamber of our own minds. Build a Team (capital T) of friends and colleagues around you who can help you stay connected to the real you. Make it a requirement of Team membership that everyone is as comfortable with your insecurity as your audacity. Now spend time with the Team on a very regular basis, no less than monthly.[26]

Focus on unleashing other people. Finally, remember what you came to do as a leader: empower other people, in both your presence and your absence. The less your agenda is about you and your shortcomings, the more the authentic version of you can show up and get the real work of leadership done.

on bereavement leave for his mother's sudden death.[c] Frances spent the rest of the summer working with the newly formed executive leadership team, which had been tasked to run the company during

c. Kalanick retained his board seat and a meaningful share of the company until he gave both up in December 2019.

the search for new leadership. Dara Khosrowshahi began his CEO tenure in September, bringing with him a track record of effectiveness at the helm of young companies.

Frances immediately began working with Khosrowshahi to continue the campaign to rebuild trust internally. Together they led an effort to rewrite the company's cultural values, one that invited input from all fifteen thousand employees on the commitments they wanted Uber to live by. A new motto they settled on was "We Do the Right Thing. Period." Other early trust wins for Khosrowshahi included strengthening relationships with regulators and executing a logic-driven focus on the services and markets that were most defensible.[27]

Most of the work we did during this period was focused on rebuilding trust at the employee level.[28] Some things were easy to identify and fix, like ratcheting down the widespread, empathy-pulverizing practice of texting during meetings *about the other people in the meeting*, a tech company norm that shocked us when we first experienced it. We introduced a new norm of turning off all personal technology and putting it away during meetings, which forced people to make eye contact with their colleagues again.

Other challenges were harder to tackle, like the need to up-skill thousands of managers. Our take was that Uber had underinvested in its people in a context of hypergrowth, leaving many managers underprepared for the increasing complexity of their jobs.[29] We addressed this logic wobble with a massive influx of executive education using a virtual, interactive classroom, which allowed us to engage employees in live case discussions—our pedagogy of choice—whether they were in San Francisco, London, or Hyderabad. Although our pilot program was voluntary and sometimes scheduled at absurdly inconvenient times in some time zones (middle of the night), six thousand Uber employees based in more than fifty countries participated in twenty-four hours of classes over sixty days. It was an extraordinary pace, scale, and absorption of management education.

The curriculum gave people tools and concepts to develop quickly as leaders—and, yes, to build more trust—while flipping a whole lot of upside-down communication triangles. Employees gained the skills not only to listen better, but also to talk in ways that made it easier to collaborate across business units and geographies. Frances also visited key global offices in her first thirty days on the job, carving out protected spaces to listen to employees and communicate leadership's commitment to build a company worthy of its people. At a time when many employees were conflicted about their Uber affiliations, Frances committed to wearing an Uber T-shirt every day until the entire company was proud to be on the payroll. (Evenings and weekends were not excluded, creating a number of awkward family moments for us, including a black-tie event.)

By the time Frances moved on from her full-time role, Uber was less wobbly.[30] There were still problems to be solved, but indicators such as employee sentiment and brand health were heading in the right direction, and the march toward an IPO began in earnest.[31] Good people were deciding to stay with the company, more good people were joining, and in what had become our favorite indicator of progress, an increasing number of Uber T-shirts could now be spotted on city streets. It was all a testament to the talent, creativity, and commitment to learning at every level of the organization—and to the foundation of trust that first Kalanick and then Khosrowshahi had been able to rebuild.

Trusting yourself

We'll talk more about Uber in the chapters ahead, particularly in chapter 6, but here's where we'll leave you in this part of the discussion: How much do you trust *yourself*? Trust is the starting point for leading others, but the path to leadership begins even earlier, with your willingness to empower yourself. What are the wobbles in that most intimate of relationships?

For example, you may not be taking care of yourself with enough *empathy* and compassion. As we explored in chapter 1, until you can reliably meet your own needs, you won't have the strength to be an effective leader and unleash anyone else. Conversely, you may lack conviction in your own *logic* and ability to perform. Finally, are you being honest with yourself about your true ambitions? Or are you hiding what really excites and inspires you behind whomever the world wants you to be? If the answer is yes or even "maybe," then you may have found the source of your *authenticity* block.

Our point is that it's not uncommon for the wobbles and anchors we experience with other people to map back to the way we feel about ourselves. Which is another reason to do this work: If you don't fully trust yourself, why should the rest of us? Once you answer that question and stabilize your trust wobbles—with both yourself and others—you get to move onto *love*, the next ring of empowerment leadership and the focus of chapter 3. There we'll explore how to create the conditions in which other people can reliably excel.

GUT CHECK

Questions for Reflection

✓ How would it impact your leadership to build more trust tomorrow than you did today?

✓ In moments when trust has broken down or failed to gain traction, which of the core drivers of trust tend to get wobbly on you: empathy, logic, or authenticity?

✓ How do stress and pressure impact your ability to build trust with others? Does your wobble change or get even wobblier?

✓ Do you lead an organization or team that needs to rebuild trust with its key stakeholders? If so, what is the institutional wobble that needs to be addressed?

✓ How will you turn your trust diagnostics into meaningful action? What can you start doing immediately to build more trust with the people around you?

3

LOVE

One of the world's first leadership scholars was a man named Valerius Maximus.[1] We're going to spend a bit of time with "ValMax" (as he's affectionately known by classical historians) since he offers us language and ideas that are remarkably relevant to challenges of empowerment leadership. We'll travel back to ancient Rome, but return to the present tense—and your own patterns as a leader—in just a few pages.

As far as we can tell, ValMax was on a mission. Troubled that only the elite got the chance to study leadership, ValMax began drafting his famous books of *Memorable Deeds and Sayings* in the late twenties CE.[2] The advice he offers in these texts is sweeping and practical—including pro tips on parenting and friendship—but he is particularly interested in teaching the rest of us how to become good magistrates and military officers. Think of him as the leadership guru of the Roman people, the Stephen Covey of the ancient world.

ValMax has a lot to say. He extolls the virtues of being "severe" and hard-hearted when circumstances demand it. A leader must be willing to exact a high price for bad behavior, he argues, as much to punish misconduct as to warn potential troublemakers. But he also devotes an entire chapter to the "fidelity of slaves," who have *some* power to determine their own destinies in ValMax's version of history.[a] He seems to be using the stories in this chapter as a crude metaphor—at least to our modern ear—for the importance of allegiance to something beyond ourselves. Taken together, ValMax's books are among the earliest written commentaries on leading a life that's, well, not about you.

High standards, deep devotion

We were blown away when we first read ValMax, as he speaks to many of the challenges modern leaders face. For example, he teaches us the value of dropping the hammer, when necessary, as a leader, as well as the importance of loyalty to mission and people. But neither behavior on its own leads to glory, and he's skeptical of both in their extremes. True leadership greatness, it turns out, is reserved for another ideal altogether, which he assigns the lofty label of "justice."

According to ValMax, justice is all about balance, about embodying multiple strengths at once, even when they feel contradictory. The leaders ValMax truly celebrates are winners, of course, but never at the cost of their integrity. They refuse to lie, cheat, or use evidence gathered through nefarious means. They preserve the dignity of their adversaries and resist the spoils of war if dishonorably won.

One of the most haunting stories he tells involves a legislator who has to decide the fate of his adulterous son. Out of respect for the father, the community wants to spare the son a gruesome

---

a. Roman slavery was a harsh, violent existence that was occasionally temporary with a defined path to freedom and even citizenship over time.

punishment—blinding in both eyes—but dad refuses to accept the charity. Instead, he gouges out one of his own eyes and one of his son's, achieving an "admirable balance . . . between compassionate father and just lawgiver."[3]

Justice seems to get much of its power from this kind of equipoise. To lead in justice means achieving a rare mix of strength and empathy, of white-hot, battle-ready ferocity blended with the cool, moderating forces of wisdom and grace. Justice is neither blindly devoted to someone else, nor so relentless in its quest for power that leaders lose their humanity. Justice neither imposes its authority at the cost of duty, nor is it dutiful at the cost of authority.

If we were to coax ValMax's observations into a modern 2×2 framework, it might look something like that in figure 3-1, with authority on one axis and duty on the other. Leaders should aim for high marks on both ideals, embodied by justice in the upper right. They should convey both commanding authority and a profound sense of duty to their fellow human beings.

FIGURE 3-1

Valerius Maximus's worldview

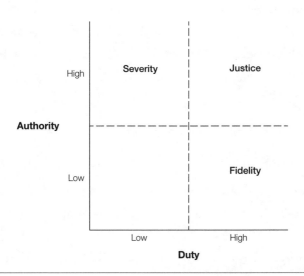

In our experience, there's truth at the heart of this worldview that's still resonant thousands of years after ValMax picked up his stylus. Leaders are most effective in empowering other people when they create a context we describe as *high standards* and *deep devotion*. When a leader's expectations are high and clear, we tend to stretch to reach them. And we are far more likely to get there when we know that leader truly has our back. It's a version of tough love that places equal emphasis on the toughness and the love. We hope to convince you, by the end of this chapter, that it's the highest form of love.

For a very current example of what we're talking about, watch Lisa Su in action. As the first female CEO of a semiconductor company, Su led the turnaround of Advanced Micro Devices (AMD), from the point of near bankruptcy to downright spectacular performance five years later.[4] She credits the clarity of her internal communications for her success (along with her mother's role modeling as an entrepreneur), but we see a clear example in Su of high standards–deep devotion leadership. One practical expression of this is her "5 percent rule," which is her commitment that AMD will get a little bit better every time the company performs a task. Demanding 50 percent improvement, she believes, is too daunting (in ValMax's language, too severe), and accepting the status quo is an unthinkably low bar. Pursuing a relentless 5 percent is exactly the right, justice-steeped balance.[5]

How do other people experience you?

Now let's explore the patterns in your own leadership behavior. First, find your comfort zone on the standards-devotion matrix in figure 3-2, the quadrant where you're most at ease operating. In this framework, we've tried to honor ValMax by using his language as inspiration for our four quadrants.[6] Which of the four tends to

FIGURE 3-2

The standards-devotion matrix

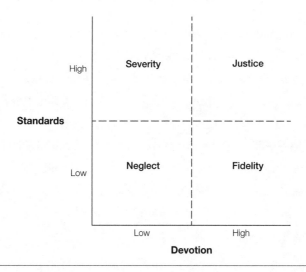

be your default position? Pick the category where people are most likely to experience you, the one that feels most natural to you.

In our experience, most of us gravitate to either fidelity or severity, displaying an opening posture of either devoted *or* tough.[7] (The psychology behind these patterns could fill another book, encompassing social norms, human development, and the biology of personality, among other rich topics.) Our conditioning would have us believe that these positions are incompatible, that there must be a trade-off between standards and devotion. It's the rare leader who defies this trade-off, casually setting the bar high while revealing deep commitment to others. The rest of us have to work our way there with healthy doses of intention.

To develop your intuition, actually draw a blank standards-devotion matrix and put a star in your default quadrant, along with a descriptor of the people who experience you this way (for example, "my sister Anita" or "new hires"). Now populate the rest of the matrix in the same way. Under what circumstances do you

Discovering Your Leadership Profile

To help you populate your standards-devotion matrix, we offer prompts below for when you may be occupying each quadrant. To be clear, there's no silent judgment embedded in this exercise. For example, someone may need your unconditional fidelity to get through a tough experience, and severity may be exactly the right response to a willful violation of your company's rules or values. Even neglect may have a strategic role to play in organizations with limited time and resources (more on this idea in chapter 5). What we're getting at here are your *patterns*—and how they may be impacting your ability to unleash other people.

> **Fidelity.** Who has a prized place in your life, but pays a low price for maintaining that position? Who gets what they want from you (status, freedom, extra dessert), with relatively few conditions placed on the exchange? Maybe it's your boss or a longtime colleague with whom you've worked for a while. Maybe it's someone who's hitting their numbers but otherwise wreaking havoc. One clue to this segment is whether you regularly protect someone from hard truths such as how others experience them.
>
> **Severity.** Who are you "toughening up" out there? Who gets the impatient version of you, the one-strike-and-you're-out you, the you with little tolerance for neediness and imperfection?

leave your comfort zone? If you're naturally in fidelity, when do you step up and bring the severity? If severity is your resting state, under what circumstances do you soften your position? Find yourself in all four quadrants and describe the patterns you observe. (See the sidebar "Discovering Your Leadership Profile.")

Maybe you're on a mission to teach someone about personal responsibility, making up for the fact that other people haven't held them fully accountable. Whatever the rationale, signs that you're settling into severity include spending a fair amount of time justifying your behavior. You don't have time to coddle any-one, right?

Neglect. Whose name do you have trouble remembering? Who have you written off as not worthy of your time and attention? You may think they don't notice your decision to relegate them to neglect (they do). In general, a crowded neglect quadrant is a red flag for both leaders and companies, so we counsel people to find ways to empty this bucket as quickly as practical. We dis-cuss how to do this with integrity later in the chapter.

Justice. Who reliably shows up around you as the best version of themselves, the one who's eager to excel and grow? And how do you feel about yourself when you're around them? This is a crucial indicator of being in justice. You feel like a superhero because, in many ways, you are one. People go higher, further, faster in your presence because they experience your conviction about what's possible for them. When do you feel like this? If it's rare, when have you *ever* felt like this?

We're making two simple points in pushing you to find your-self in all of the quadrants. The first is that *you have it in you.* We all have the ability to foster a range of emotional contexts for the people in our lives. This is important when we move on to the chal-lenge of going from one quadrant to another. There's no place on this framework you can't go; indeed, you're already familiar with the landscape. Our second point is that from the standpoint of empowerment leadership, not all quadrants are created equal. If you want to unleash people, then spending most of your time in justice is much more effective than the other three options.

We've done this exercise with thousands of leaders, and a typical self-assessment looks something like figure 3-3.

In this example, a C-level tech leader we were coaching (we'll call him "John") realized that his default position was severity. John easily set the bar high, but often held back his devotion, which had earned him a companywide reputation for being "cold." With his direct reports, however, it was different. He was able to combine clear expectations with deep commitment, resulting in a highly empowered, high-performing team.

In doing this exercise, John realized that the reporting structure was a factor. It was part of his job description to develop his team, and the collaborative nature of the work created plenty of oppor-

FIGURE 3-3

How do other people experience you?

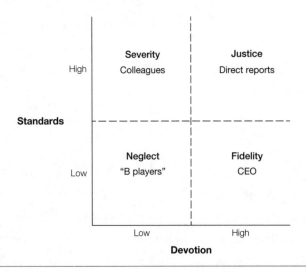

tunities to reveal devotion. But the structure was a mental barrier for him with everyone else. Without an explicit mandate to develop the rest of the company, John found himself in severity. In addition, while he was loyal to the CEO to whom he reported, he also sometimes slipped into a "yes-man" relationship with her. His deference to his boss's authority got in the way of telling her what he really thought and becoming a rigorous thought partner.

Finally, John acknowledged that he sometimes unfairly dismissed people he coded as "B players." And while a few may have earned their exile to neglect, John's judgment was a blunt instrument. Colleagues often shut down in response to his swift, nonverbal verdicts, even when they had something valuable to contribute.

The journey to justice for leaders like John involves resisting the gravitational pull of our leadership conditioning, the part of us that worries that if we reveal more devotion, then we'll also have to somehow lower our standards. Nothing could be further from the truth, which we're going to help you visualize by introducing you to Carlos Rodriguez-Pastor.

The Notorious CRP

Carlos Rodriguez-Pastor is a self-made billionaire in Peru who has played a pivotal role in supporting and enabling the country's emerging middle class. His company, Intercorp, touches nearly every part of Peruvian life, from banks to supermarkets to schools. "CRP," as he's lovingly known, is the living, breathing embodiment of high standards and deep devotion. CRP sets sky-high standards, while maintaining absolute devotion to everyone in his expansive orbit.

It starts with a rigorous selection process. Interviewing with CRP is a famously drawn-out experience, comprising what feels like endless rounds of meetings, often outside the office, where he believes people are more likely to reveal who they really are. He is quick to put candidates "in the freezer" if he thinks they're using connections to get hired. While the concept of a meritocracy has become confused in many sectors, CRP's merit-based culture is among the healthiest we've observed.

If CRP does have a bias, it's for entrepreneurial personalities who find ways to achieve more with less. He gravitates toward people who reveal hard-earned grit and a hunger to improve themselves. One year he famously rewarded his top performers with an invitation to join him in climbing a mountain near Mt. Everest. The more-senior executives purchased business-class tickets to fly in comfort on the multileg trip from Lima to Nepal. In classic CRP style, he offered a last-minute invitation to anyone flying coach to join him on his private plane for the journey, a story that spread quickly throughout the company. Everyone got the message: for CRP, status doesn't mean access.

CRP's most defining trait may be his unshakable belief in what's possible for the people around him, from his colleagues to his fellow Peruvian citizens. CRP believes that human beings are the only truly competitive asset, and he invests in people with unapologetic audacity. His employees can earn no-strings-attached scholarships to top schools, and intensive education is baked into the job design of everyone on his team. Even his most senior leaders must complete rigorous coursework, and CRP expects his team to approach this work with as much intensity as the rest of their jobs. He often sits in on classes himself, taking detailed notes on his employees' participation and then huddling with faculty to review those notes at the end of sessions. For context, we've taught countless classes to executive audiences and have never seen another CEO do this.

Remarkably, CRP is almost never alone, at least not when he's working. Someone else is always by his side, typically a rotating cast of young leaders, invited to learn from direct exposure to his approach. He regularly moves people around business units for the developmental value of operating in new contexts, and he hosts an annual learning trip where managers travel to a foreign country simply to learn. The trip is designed to expose his team to how fast the world is changing, at a speed that means they're almost always behind someone else. He describes the trip as "our annual vaccine against complacency."

In short, CRP refuses to miss a teachable moment. One day, in perhaps our favorite example of the lengths to which he'll go to communicate expectations, CRP purposely went to the office wearing a pair of clown bloomers under his suit pants that he revealed "accidentally." He went about his day soberly, participating in meetings, working with his team—with red and white polka dots pouring out of his waistband. No one dared to say anything. At the end of the day, he rounded up everyone with whom he had interacted and said, "I'm now questioning whether you should be on my team." No one lost their job, but CRP made it clear how much he valued the truth, regardless of hierarchy or power differences.

Once he's convinced by someone's potential, CRP is all in, particularly with people who share his values and ambition for equitable change. CRP's goal is nothing less than the country's economic transformation, and development indicators suggest he's on his way.[8] This development ethos comes to life at scale in his Innova Schools project, an innovative network of private, K–12 schools he designed and funded. Innova Schools deliver exceptional results at a fraction of the cost of public schools in the developed world, a business model designed to address the crisis of access to quality education in Peru. At last count, Innova had opened fifty-five schools—fifty-four in Peru and one in Mexico—serving more than forty-three thousand students. It's now on track to become the largest private school network in the region.

The young people coming out of these schools are primed to build the future that CRP envisions. One recent Innova graduate we learned about—her dad drives taxis and mom sells pastries at the local market—saw an ad in the local newspaper about Peru Champs, a scholarship program for bright kids who want to enroll at Innova Schools but can't afford it. The student competed with hundreds of other kids for a spot and passed with flying colors. Soon after, she enrolled at the school in Santa Clara, a low-income area on the outskirts of Lima where many families from the Andes have migrated.

At first, this young woman was intimidated by her new environment, feeling out of place in a school that charges an aspirational fee of $100 a month and caters to an emerging middle class she was far from joining. Over time, she thrived and ultimately graduated at the top of her class. She chose to apply to the best schools in the world for college, applying to institutions that could put her on a path to becoming a world-class neuroscientist. In April 2019, she became the first ever Innova Schools graduate to be admitted to Dartmouth, NYU, Swarthmore, Georgetown, Tufts, Emory, Oxford, and Stanford. Innova has offered her a full scholarship to pursue her studies. No strings attached.

CRP's ultimate dream is to empower Peru. He believes that if the people around him, like the path-breaking Innova graduate, become strong leaders in their own right, they will invest their talent back into the country, spurring a virtuous cycle that will unleash the potential of an entire nation. He's already seeing parts of this dream become a reality, as dynamism and activity in Peru's most important service sectors continue to grow. Many of the leaders he has developed and launched are now building vital businesses of their own, continuing CRP's transformative tradition of high standards and deep devotion.

Leadership in motion

Given the mission of this book, the pattern we care most about is this: most of us are not like Carlos Rodriguez-Pastor, practicing high standards–deep devotion leadership almost casually at this point. Instead, we're often spending less time in justice than our leadership mandate asks of us. We're sometimes creating empowering contexts where other people can succeed wildly; at other times, we're either not helpful or making choices that undermine their ability to thrive. Our thoughts and emotions distract us from leadership. It becomes about us rather than them.

Said differently, most of us hit the justice target when it's emotionally convenient. We embrace justice when the conditions are optimal—when we've slept well, or we're not under pressure, or when it doesn't require too much discomfort or deviation from our preferred patterns of behavior—but this convergence of circumstances rarely coincides with our biggest opportunities to lead.

The thing that will matter most, hands down, to your ability to empower others is the capacity to move into justice *whenever it will make a difference*. How do you achieve that level of control? How do you travel, on your terms and timeline, from severity or fidelity or even neglect all the way into justice? It's the ultimate leadership journey and the focus of the rest of this chapter. It turns out that leaders and scholars—including ValMax—have been wrestling with this question for thousands of years.

Forget who you are

There is healthy agreement among leadership practitioners about the first step on any developmental path, which is to start by letting go of strict assumptions about who you are and, more importantly, who you are *not*. Get yourself into a frame of mind where you're willing to challenge the rules you've written for yourself about the stark lines and limits of your identity.

As you may have discovered in the chapter's opening exercise, identity is often more pliable than we think. When it comes to leadership, we tend to have patterns and preferences, but it's rare that we're truly stuck—inflexibly severe, for example, or uncritically devoted. Indeed, we tend to have it in ourselves to be everywhere on the standards-devotion matrix, to be the dismissive, apathetic blockhead in the meeting and the most inspiring general on the competitive battlefield.

Your leadership past does not define your future, and therein lies the possibility. Writing about the dynamism of circumstance and identity, ValMax urges his readers to look closely at the lives of the leaders they admire. Many had undistinguished starts in life, if not downright grim ones. But they persevered and turned challenges into gifts, pulling glory from the crucible of adversity.[9]

At one point, ValMax offers a startlingly modern "best self" metaphor for Sulla, a famous statesman and general and one of the most colorful characters in ValMax's writings. Sulla's worst self—on flamboyant display in his early years—was marked by self-indulgence and self-distraction. His disciplined best self, in contrast, delivered countless battlefield victories for Rome in the name of something bigger than himself. ValMax concludes there was a great leader lurking inside Sulla all along, just waiting to scatter the "bars . . . by which it was confined."[10]

We all possess this type of character strength, the strength to break free from whatever leadership identities we've chosen to occupy in the past. It's simply a decision about whether to use that power—and where to go with your newfound freedom.

From devotion to love

On her quest to teach the world about the merits of a "growth mindset," Professor Carol Dweck has grown comfortable with tough conversations. She's chosen to get in the face of parents and educators worldwide to let us know—in clear but loving terms—that we're holding kids back with all of our good intentions. Among other behaviors, Dweck wants us to stop praising our children in ways that do more harm than good.

At some point on our journey to becoming passable parents, both starting deep in the fidelity camp, we were exposed to Dweck's research. She advises focusing on a child's effort ("you worked so hard!"), something within their control, rather than innate traits ("you're so smart!") that ratchet up the stakes of failure and under- mine the drive to take risks and improve. Crucially, Dweck's approach allows you to raise the bar without trading off a shred of devotion.[11]

In our worldview, Dweck is the embodiment of justice, on a mis- sion to broadcast the price of fidelity. The punchline, of course, is that fidelity is going to cost you. To remain in a high-commitment, low-standards posture as a leader allows you to *feel* as if you're in service of others, since you're taking care of them, but it's mostly about you. It's a decision to trade off other people's excellence in order to stay within the limits of your own emotional safety zone.

Dweck summarized her challenge with the following questions: Are you preparing the child for the path? Or the path for the child? Our translation to leadership is this: Are you asking your people to evolve? Or are you instead—because of loyalty or complacency or conflict avoidance—asking relatively little of them? Are you empowering others or are you making them comfortable?

If people feel supported but unmotivated around you, cozy but passive, then your path to justice involves raising the bar. Let Dweck's prep-for-the-path challenge be your battle cry—a reminder of the Sulla within all of us, waiting to break free.

Catch them doing something right

There are countless ways to raise expectations, some more or less of a stretch for longtime fidelity occupants. The trick is to reject the flawed assumption that in order to move the goalposts, you have to give up any of that beautiful devotion.

The good news is that the most effective mechanism we know for accelerating human progress taps into our natural devotional impulses. The idea is simple: catch someone in the act of behaving exactly as you want them to behave, using sincere and specific praise. Describe the behavior in enough detail so that they can replicate it. Take it from Dweck and focus on things that a person can truly control. Rinse and repeat on a very regular basis.

The specific part matters a lot. Sincere but *non*specific praise is easier to dispense, but it rarely helps someone improve, since they're not entirely sure how to recreate the magic. For example, telling someone they did a "nice job" after a meeting generally doesn't help, since the recipient has to guess what they did to earn it. In contrast, telling someone, "The way you took two competing ideas and articulated what was in common between them was really effective in breaking the stalemate," has enough detail so that the listener knows what to do more of the next time. Another word for this, of course, is positive reinforcement.

Positive reinforcement can feel awkward at first, as it's a departure from prevailing feedback norms. (If you took our other people's awesomeness [OPA] challenge in chapter 1, then you have a running start.) Within about two weeks of practice, however, people consistently report back to us that it begins to feel natural and also refreshingly, delightfully *good*. It forces you to pay closer attention to the people around you and generates a positive charge between you. You get to be the Santa Claus of feedback, handing out improvement gifts wherever you go.

Regrettably, much of the feedback culture in organizations today is downright Scrooge-like. Feedback tends to be vague and mostly negative. One particularly ineffective manager we observed had a habit of sending two-word emails that said, "not good." Literally, that was the entire email. Not surprisingly, this behavior created mild-to-intense anxiety among her colleagues, with little hope of improving anything.

There's still a time and place to correct negative behaviors, but we advise doing so sparingly, as it's much less effective at spurring improvement.[12] When you do have to do it, bring evidence to the discussion. Be clear about the future state you envision and the higher-order reasons for it. Whenever possible, frame the behavior change as a small pivot with a big payoff to your shared mission. Let's call this type of intervention "constructive advice."

For the feedback Scrooges among us, this next part is important: for constructive advice to be credible, it must be layered on top of a foundation of trust. Of course, that foundation requires empathy— the recipient's conviction that you're truly seeing them, both the good stuff and the bad. (If someone only sees what's wrong with us, then we tend to process what they say as judgment rather than as fuel for improvement.) In the absence of empathy, constructive advice can easily become destructive, making the recipient worse rather than better. For example, it could make them more self-conscious in their execution or less confident in their decision making. Note that this happens *all the time*.

Somehow an assumption has taken hold in many companies that "real" feedback is the negative stuff, the difficult conversations that we all need to learn how to have with each other. Positive reinforcement, in contrast, is something to be tolerated suspiciously on the way to getting to all this realness. In our experience, the very opposite is true. It's positive reinforcement that gets the job done, the most powerful accelerant we've observed for helping human beings scramble up a learning curve.

If you want more data, observe the training of well-behaved dogs. We suggest the legendary Pawsitive Dog training center in Boston, founded and led brilliantly by Jenifer Vickery. On any given day in the center, most of the dogs are doing things humans find difficult, such as lounging peacefully, untethered, in the presence of constant stimulation. Watch the methods of Vickery and her team closely. Are the dogs getting rewarded for good behavior or corrected for bad? At what ratios? The headline is that the dogs that are thriving are being lavished with a constant flow of food and attention, in response to very specific behaviors the trainers want to encourage. We'd argue that this approach works for most creatures, goldfish and above in biological complexity.

There's a role for both positive reinforcement and constructive advice in anyone's evolution, but here's the part that surprises most people: the right ratio of positive to constructive is *at least* 5:1. For every unit of constructive advice you decide to hand out, the recipient should ideally receive five units of positive reinforcement. Many of the workplace cultures we've studied are closer to 1:5, with far more effort going toward behavior correction, only some of it constructive.

We've seen firsthand that a 5:1 positive-to-negative ratio is within anyone's reach, even the die-hard constructive advice givers. If you give constructive advice once or twice a week, for example, look for daily opportunities for sincere, specific, positive reinforcement. Monthly constructive advice? Shoot for the positive stuff slightly more than weekly. And so on. You get the math. Once you get hooked on the uptick in improvement, we're confident you'll be converted.

How will you know if you're getting it right? Your performance metric is someone else's improvement. If you're not seeing improvement, then it's *your* job to try another way. Restate your observations with more specificity. Build more trust so that your recipient(s) can actually hear what you have to say. You don't get credit for trying regardless of whether you were effective. Your job as a leader is to make others better. If the feedback you're giving has a neutral to negative impact, then you're not doing your job. (See the sidebar "Ten Ways to Set Higher Standards Tomorrow.")

From expectations to love

Some of us are most comfortable as leaders in severity. If that describes you, let's assume you got there for good reasons. Revealing high standards but minimal devotion might serve a productive, short-term purpose for the herd (e.g., making a negative example of someone), but for a leader to stay there is a pricey choice for most teams.

Like the trade-offs associated with fidelity, to stay in severity is a decision that's driven primarily by your own needs, particularly the need for control and security. Severity can meet these needs, at least provisionally, but its upside is limited. Other people tend to give you what you ask for, but rarely much more than that. They exert just enough energy to avoid feelings of failure or shame or whatever your management weapon of choice may be, but it's often too risky around leaders in severity to innovate or deviate from expectations (even if it's to exceed them).

The counterexample, some would argue, is Steve Jobs. At times notoriously severe as a leader—arrogant, bullying, impatient—Jobs built the most sustainably innovative company of the last century. But we don't see Jobs as a severity success story. From our perspective, Jobs was at his most effective when he paired high (if blunt) standards with unflinching devotion to the potential of his team. He regularly empowered the people around him to perform superhuman tasks, and they responded with fierce loyalty, even at the height of the war for tech talent. Debi Coleman, an executive on the team that launched the first Macintosh, summarized the feeling of many of his top lieutenants: "I consider myself the absolute luckiest person in the world to have worked with him."[13]

One of our favorite Jobs anecdotes is recounted by Walter Isaacson, who wrote the definitive biography of the iconic leader. He

Ten Ways to Set Higher Standards Tomorrow

What else can you do to quickly raise the bar for the people around you? Here are some of our favorite approaches, all achievable within the next twenty-four hours:

1. **Make it a group project.** If fidelity is your jam, one painless way to get started is to raise the *collective* standard. Gather your team and describe the team's goals and the *why* of your new expectations. Decide together how you'll achieve your shared goals and how the team wants to be held accountable for delivering.

2. **Celebrate a win.** Take that positive reinforcement machine out for a real test drive. Publicly praise someone for doing exactly what you want them to do, using the magic of sincere and specific praise. Make it clear to everyone listening precisely what they have to do to get their own "Scooby Snacks" from you (our preferred term, as inspired by the rewards-motivated cartoon dog).

3. **Treat someone like their better, future self.** Don't just stay open to the idea that someone might one day evolve: assume they've already done so. Engage with a new and improved version of someone, even if they're not quite there yet. For example, give them that stretch assignment you've been holding back or offer advice that only their better self can execute. Anything to signal that the future is now.

4. **Put your high performers to work.** Ask the high performers on your team to help you raise the bar by coaching and inspiring

their colleagues. This type of mentoring can take lots of forms, from group meetings to intensive one-on-one work. Give your new coaching squad the flexibility to interpret their mandate in ways that will energize them.

5. **Convene an after-action review.** This is the US Army's formal protocol for learning from what actually happened. Do your own version by getting your colleagues together to discuss what you could have done better as a team, even when things went well. Just the act of setting this agenda allows you to communicate that the status quo isn't good enough.

6. **Set better goals.** Great work is being done to codify and share the world's learning on goal setting. Get smart about this movement and adapt it to your own context. One of our favorite tools is the OKR (objectives and key results) system used by Intel, Google, and others. And if you want to get started even faster, consider taking the SMART approach, which calls for goals to be specific, measurable, achievable, relevant, and time bound.

7. **Broadcast your ambition.** Tell everyone around you what you're trying to achieve, at a level of detail that makes sense for the relationship. Make your audacity and sense of purpose infectious. If recruiting accountability partners will help you succeed, then don't be shy. Find a peer (or two, or three) to keep you honest.

(continued)

8. **Eliminate an inefficiency.** Make it clear that time is too valuable to waste. Discover what people dread doing and reduce their pain. Easy wins in most organizations include streamlining reporting and optimizing performance reviews, but stay humble and curious in this process. Assume you don't know everything that's draining your team's time or all of the latest tools that could help.

9. **Take bold action.** Take immediate, meaningful action toward a personal or team goal—the bolder the action, the better. Ideally, do something you've never done before, something that surprises even your closest colleagues. Make it clear that beliefs and norms have changed, starting with you.

10. **Be the standard.** Model the standards and behaviors you want the people around you to adopt. Be impatient with your own mediocrity and don't let yourself off the hook. If you find yourself slipping, take a timeout from the leadership path. Spend some time recovering until you're back on track.

tells the story of Jobs trying to get the glass on the first iPhone right, which he believed the company Corning had the ability to manufacture. Jobs flew to meet with the CEO of Corning, Wendell Weeks, who informed him that his request was impossible, certainly in the time frame Jobs needed, since Corning hadn't made the glass since the 1960s. "Don't be afraid," Jobs replied, to a fellow corporate titan he hardly knew. "You can do it. Get your mind around it. You can do it." An astonished Weeks figured out how to retrofit his Kentucky factory and delivered the glass in under six months. To this day, the glass on iPhones and iPads is manufactured by Corning.[14]

In this exchange with Weeks, Jobs made the fundamental choice that all leaders have to make, to choose "me" or "you" or, in our worldview, to choose fear or love. Instead of dismissing Weeks, he made him feel like a hero, someone capable of achieving the impossible. In our experience, this is not as hard as it sounds. Many leaders already *are* deeply devoted to the people around them; they're just not effectively communicating that devotion. They're rooting for their people in the quiet—and safety—of their own hearts, keeping their humanity to themselves, where it isn't doing anyone much good. The journey from severity to justice is often about finding ways to reveal your true commitment. There are innumerable ways to do this, and we call out some of our favorites in the sidebar "Ten Ways to Reveal Deep Devotion Tomorrow."

From neglect (all the way) to love

When you find yourself in neglect, you essentially have two choices: invest in the relationship or respectfully sever it. Staying in neglect with people is generally a toxic choice, for you and everyone else. There *is* such a thing as benign neglect, but it's a high beta strategy, as likely to produce disastrous outcomes as positive ones.

One pattern of neglect we see is the subconscious decision to disregard someone who needs to be separated but is still in the ecosystem. As creatures of feeling, we often insulate ourselves from the discomfort of the separation process by dehumanizing a person, sometimes even in small ways like reduced eye contact. See the sidebar "How to Respectfully Fire Someone" for a

Ten Ways to Reveal Deep Devotion Tomorrow

The following are ten things that you can do to communicate commitment to the people in your life, all achievable within the next twenty-four hours:

1. **Again, put down your phone.** In a world of relentless, device-driven distraction, giving someone your undiluted attention is among your clearest devotion signals. Use your devices as they were meant to be used, to get closer to people at a distance instead of further away from the people right next to you.

2. **Channel your inner Terry Gross.** Get curious about the lives being lived around you. Why have your colleagues made the choices they made? What has surprised or delighted or disappointed them along the way? If you're stuck for how to begin the conversation, kick things off with the a line favored by iconic public radio host Terry Gross: "Tell me about yourself."[15]

3. **Experience their reality.** Assuming you know what your colleagues do all day is a fairly common severity stance, along with concluding that it's probably not the right things. Find out the truth with active inquiry or even some good, old-fashioned job shadowing. If they're spending their time in ways that are indeed less than optimal, help them to prioritize better.

4. **Ask how you can help.** Find out how to be of service to someone. Don't muddy the agenda with other things on your to-do list; keep the conversation focused on how you can help someone achieve something meaningful. And don't end the

conversation until you've committed to take action in ways that improve their chance of success.

5. **Proactively help (without the asking part).** Pick someone on your team whose proverbial "plate" you know well (ideally, because you've piled things onto it) and surprise them by removing something. Show them you get it by choosing something that's causing particular frustration and/or is misaligned with their long-term goals.

6. **Offer snacks.** Feed people, preferably something they actually want to eat, but even a surprise box of doughnut holes will do the trick. To feed someone is to acknowledge their presence and humanity at the most foundational level. An edible offering can be wrapped in all kinds of packaging—celebration, gratitude, sustenance for a hard night ahead—that transforms easily into the currency of devotion.

7. **Give them a break.** The research is clear that sprints only work when they're combined with time for recovery. Protect the space for real recovery for people, especially those who think they're the bionic exception, who think they can keep going indefinitely without stopping to rest. It's even simpler for those who report to you: make it non-negotiable and send them home for the day (or longer).

8. **Acknowledge their lives outside work.** Recognition of someone's multidimensional existence can show up in many forms, so, no, you don't have to feign interest in their toddler's

(continued)

Spiderman-themed party. Instead, you can simply operate under the assumption that they *have* a life outside work by minimizing evening and weekend work. This is particularly meaningful to women, who are more likely to be primary caretakers of children and aging parents.

9. **Offer sincere, specific gratitude.** Thank someone for doing something that truly made your life better. Be specific about the act and its effects, how their decision made a difference. For a bigger devotion bang, send a thank-you note or another tangible expression of your gratitude. There's no shame in being unoriginal here. "Stop with the flowers," said no one ever.

10. **Less me, more we.** Language matters, in ways that can shape—and reshape—our realities. As a starting place, check the number of "I" and "me" statements you're making over the course of the day. Replace a healthy percentage of them with "we" and "us." For bonus points, throw in more "you" and "yours," as in, "How can we help you achieve your hopes and dreams?"

broader discussion on how to terminate someone with integrity, which it will not surprise you to hear, requires a move into justice.

The path from neglect to justice can feel like a long one, but like many of the choices that transform our experience, it can be traversed in an instant. It turns out the decision to see someone takes no time at all.

How to Respectfully Fire Someone

Over the last decade, we have worked with countless senior executives, many of them in challenging circumstances. Regret is rarely their primary emotion, but when it does show up, it's almost always regret at not moving fast enough to do something they knew was right for their business. In the vast majority of those cases, the thing they waited too long to do was to let someone go who was no longer right for the company.

The ability to quickly and gracefully part ways with employees is among your most important tactical leadership skills. Here's our advice for how to do it with high standards and deep devotion for everyone involved:

Recognize the pain of the status quo. Start with a full and honest accounting of the costs of inaction. Most leaders are aware of the downside of an underperforming employee (for example, their impact on performance or culture), but they underestimate the upside of having the right person in the role. What would true excellence in this function do for your team or company? How would it change your business?

Preserve their dignity. Anyone getting fired is going to feel some pain, in most cases, emotionally and financially. Protect their dignity however you can, from the timing of the discussion, to the separation package, to the exit protocol you follow. If you can avoid involving security, please do. Somehow it became standard practice to make separated employees feel like criminals, and yet rarely does the retaliation risk justify the humiliation we extract on their way out the door.

Do it yourself. Do not outsource the discussion to someone else on your team. Your people are paying close attention to how this goes down, and it's a chance to send clear signals about accountability and values—both the company's and your own—and to also make sure the person being separated is properly supported. Those opportunities can be easily squandered if you're not in the room.

Commit to their future success. Be honest about your decision and consider framing it in ways that help them find their next opportunity. Give them the organizational context. Thank them for the contributions they *did* make. Everyone stumbles at some point in their career, and in most separation cases, there's no reason you can't play a role in helping them get back up. There may be complicating factors, but whatever the situation allows you to do, be generous.

Honor everyone else. Make sure the team members that stay behind are getting sufficient attention. What does your decision mean for them? What conclusions should they draw from it? Although some tension may be healthy at this point, have a plan for reducing unproductive anxiety. Answer whatever questions you can, quickly and ideally in person. Then get your legions back out on the battlefield, focused on advancing the larger mission.

By any other name

We were originally going to name this chapter "Tough Love" but decided simply on "Love." The gift of helping someone reach for a better future than the present they're living is among the purest forms of human love we know. It's certainly the one that gets us up in the morning.

Part of the reason we use the word "gift" is because it's not free: to make others better comes at a price for the giver. As we've explored throughout this chapter, there's no path into justice that doesn't involve some amount of tension for you as a leader. When you're doing this right, when you're making the kinds of changes that enable other people to thrive, you may feel as if you're out over your skis at some point. Our message to you, to all of us, is to tuck your head and keep going. Get comfortable with the discomfort. The payoff is a force with enough power to unleash other people, a force conventionally known as love.

And whenever you're ready, move on to the next ring of empowerment leadership: belonging. This is where you get to empower not only individuals, but also the unit of teams, ensuring that everyone can contribute their unique capacities and perspectives. It's where diversity and inclusion create the path—the *freeway*, more accurately—to truly exceptional performance.

GUT CHECK

Questions for Reflection

- ✓ What do other people tend to feel when they're around you? What do you *want* them to feel?

- ✓ Where do you naturally find yourself in the standards-devotion matrix? Which quadrant is most comfortable for you?

- ✓ What do you need to do differently as a leader to consistently occupy the justice quadrant? To reveal high standards and deep devotion simultaneously?

- ✓ What makes doing the work to be in justice worth it to you? What will change when you can reliably set other people up to thrive?

4

BELONGING

We're not here to make the case for diversity and inclusion. Yes, that case still needs to be made in some organizations or, to be more precise, still needs to be better understood and more widely embraced. If you or someone you love is in this camp, convinced that inclusion is a nice-to-have management luxury, to be prioritized only after you solve more important business problems, then we will first refer you to the fantastic scholarship on the competitive advantage and moral imperative of being a champion for difference. One headline is that true inclusion—not just diversity—will help you solve those business problems *faster* and *better.*[1]

As we began to explore in our chapter on trust, organizations win when people can bring their complete, multidimensional selves to work. And it's not just underrepresented employees who benefit. We are all better off in inclusive spaces where authenticity can flourish. This chapter takes that observation as a given and explores your next set of challenges: the practical tasks of building and leading inclusive teams.

Our goal is to help you empower teams that excel, not in spite of their differences, but *because* of them. Many good leaders we know are committed to this idea but are still having a hard time getting it done and fully unleashing people who don't look and think and talk like them. This chapter is about how to overcome this dynamic.[a]

Begin at the beginning (and everywhere else)

We break up our discussion according to the traditional human resources life cycle, meaning the phases through which someone experiences your organization. Starting with the recruitment of new employees, we then move on to creating spaces where everyone has an opportunity to thrive and advance, and then close with retaining great people. We look at these challenges through the lens of empowerment leadership that makes being different not only safe but also welcome, celebrated, and cherished.

To be clear, this is meant to be an intuitive structure, not our suggested order of operations. Our advice is to do—or at least to *start* doing—as much as you can simultaneously. When people ask us about the optimal timing for inclusive change, our standard response is, "How about now?"

First, there's a strong, rip-off-the-Band-Aid argument for simply getting on with things. Anticipation of change introduces anxiety into an ecosystem, and the antidote is to replace it with *actual* change. The longer you wait, the more space the human imagination has to hallucinate—a favorite term of our friend and fellow educator Tom

---

a. We disproportionately focus on women and LGBT+ perspectives in this chapter, as stand-ins for differences that are visible and (mostly) invisible. This choice reflects both our space limitations and our particular experience navigating the world as members of these two groups. Needless to say, only some of our advice is transferable to other populations, but we still hope it remains directionally useful, regardless of the type of difference you seek to support. Wherever practical, we broaden the discussion.

DeLong—about all the catastrophic turns the future could take. Getting started also allows you to create enough momentum to help you up the inevitable learning curve and around whatever resistance you may meet along the way.

Here's the main problem with *not* doing as much as you can, as quickly as you can, to promote inclusion: failing to act in the presence of bias is demoralizing and inhumane. Once you've identified systemic barriers to the contributions of your fellow human beings, delays can be interpreted as comfort with their inequity and unrealized potential. Imagine saying something like this to your colleagues: "Look, it's come to our attention that we're only empowering the straight, white men on the team, but we have a lot on our plate right now, so we're going to wait until later to deal with it." That's essentially what you're communicating when you move slowly in response to unveiled bias.

There will always be people telling you to slow down and do less. Always, always, always. They often have long institutional memories, care deeply about the organization, and worry most about the good things that may be lost in a transformative change process. When we took on gender inequalities at Harvard Business School (more on this in chapter 6), well-meaning colleagues who believed they were acting in the school's best interest advised us to wait a year. One year didn't seem like much to ask for a hundred-year-old institution.

In our experience, it's everything to ask. We've learned the hard way that big organizational change almost always happens quickly, so our advice is to start now and slay all the dragons you can find. We've partnered closely with change makers at every level, and we've never heard anyone say, "I wish we had taken longer and done less." Indeed, we frequently hear the opposite. (See the sidebar "Ten Signs Your Organization Is Stalling.")

Ten Signs Your Organization Is Stalling

Let's say you're making progress toward a more inclusive operating environment, but you suspect your colleagues are trying to slow you down. Resistance to change can show up in many forms, some of them hard to decipher. The following ten signs reveal that your organization is digging in its heels:

1. **A task force has been assigned to the problem.** A small, intrepid team of reformers is one thing; indeed, it's among the most important tools for accelerating action. Most task forces, it turns out, do not fit this profile. If your organization is pushing you to rely on a structure like this that's outside the typical chain of command, make sure it's a mechanism with the legitimacy and decision rights to make a difference.

2. **You're being thanked for your time and effort.** If you suspect you're being indulged and dismissed, then you probably are. By the way, this is not the same thing as being disagreed with, which is a perfectly acceptable response to you. Your obligation as a change maker is to make the persuasive case for your ideas. Your colleagues' obligation is to engage with them in good faith, not to meet all of your demands.

3. **People doubt whether the organization (really) has a problem.** Be prepared for your colleagues to push back on the diagnosis that the company has an inclusion problem. Hard truths are, by definition, difficult to face, and this is particularly true for data that confirm a tolerance for bias (or worse). Stay strong. Be fluent in the evidence you've gathered and also in resonant stories about the cost of barriers to everyone's full participation.

4. **You're asked to respond to the grave concerns of unidentified critics.** These exchanges often start with some variation on, "As your friend, I think you should know what people are saying." This is usually a tactic to keep you in check rather than empower you with information. Don't take the bait and react to rumor and hearsay. Encourage your critics to reveal themselves so that you can engage directly with their concerns, which may very well be valid. Collaboration happens in daylight.

5. **The specter of "legal issues" is being invoked.** The antidote to this one is to work directly with the legal team, which is often made up of people who are far more creative, flexible, and solutions oriented than the detractors who are using their name. Lawyers are rarely the risk-intolerant killjoys they're made out to be by non-lawyers, so partner with them early.

6. **Your colleagues point out all the *other* things that are changing.** This critique assumes there's some kind of measurable limit on a firm's capacity to absorb positive change—and you're getting dangerously close to that line. People tend to underestimate their company's capacity to adapt to a better reality, as well as the true cost of continued inaction. We'll say it again, for the absence of doubt: failing to act in the presence of bias is demoralizing and inhumane.

7. **You keep hearing about a future state where the conditions for change will be much, much better.** This may be the most common expression of resistance we see, the fantasy that it's going to be easier to change things at some point in the future. In our

(continued)

experience, this is almost never the case, and the opposite is usually true. The clarity and momentum you have right now are tremendous assets, but they're also perishable ones. In most cases, the "fierce urgency of now" wins the day, particularly when the well-being of the people around you is on the line.

8. **The timeline for action is growing.** This is another common delay tactic, a proposed antidote to the concerns expressed in numbers six and seven. Your ideas are embraced at a conceptual level, but the timetable for change keeps being extended. Treat this development as an existential threat to your mission. When it comes to promoting inclusion—a mission so critical to the health of your organization—the right time to act is now.

9. **Your colleagues think they can wait you out.** Management thought leader Earl Sasser calls this "kidney stone management," the assumption that this too shall pass. Make it absolutely clear that you're not going anywhere, preferably with a smile. If it takes showing up at someone's office door with a cup of coffee (just the way they like it) every morning until you get the meeting, then so be it. That tactic, by the way, has never failed us.

10. **You keep hearing, "We've already tried that."** Some version of your proposed actions may have been tried before. If so, do the work to understand that history. Figure out whether the strategy or execution of past efforts was flawed and learn as much as possible from whatever went wrong. Regardless, context changes, including the very material context of your willingness to lead on these issues. *You* haven't tried before, which can make all the difference.

Step one: Attract and select diverse talent

Every recruitment process we've observed up close could be improved in some way to better promote diversity. Our goal is to give you permission to pursue this improvement with the same enthusiasm and analytic rigor you bring to other organizational challenges. Start by framing it as a problem, the same way losing market share or operational inefficiency is a problem. It may be more emotionally charged than other problems, but in order to solve it, you need to get past that charge and into a resourceful, can-do state.

Lots of organizations experience some variation on this reality: they've learned how to recruit the best people from a narrow demographic, but struggle beyond that profile. For example, many US companies lament the fact that they've had terrific success attracting straight, white men they know, but have not yet learned how to reliably recruit women, people of color, LGBT+ people, any intersectional combination therein, or the straight, white men they *don't* know. (By "know" we mean people who are separated by one or two degrees and largely share the same networks, influences, and life experiences.) Here's a simple, directional test: if the demographics of your team don't bear much resemblance to the demographics of the broader population, then you may be in this camp. You've likely put artificial barriers on the talent pools in which you're fishing, which means not only are you missing out on the rest of that beautiful pond of humanity, but you're also at risk of a culture of conformity.

Recruitment has two parts to it, attraction and selection. *Attraction* means the ability to create outside interest in working at your organization. If your existing processes tend to attract a singular profile, then you likely need to design *different* processes for attracting other profiles. It doesn't mean you have to blow everything up. You may very well be able to keep your existing practices in place for recruiting the original profile since your system seems to be working there.

Here's what *different* tends to look like when it comes to attraction: identify the profiles you're missing and recruit in places where they tend to gather. For example, if you're an organization that skews white and male in its leadership ranks and you're now looking for legal talent, start with organizations like 1844, an association of successful black lawyers.[b] If you're looking for technical talent, attend the Grace Hopper Celebration, which bills itself as "the world's largest gathering of women technologists."[2] Begin actively recruiting at historically black colleges and universities. And women's colleges. And colleges in geographies that are unfamiliar to you. Said differently, if you want to attract different types of people, then start meeting them where they are, in different types of places (ideally, where they're the majority).

Cammie Dunaway is the charismatic chief marketing officer of Duolingo, the breakthrough language-learning app that's known for its heavy use of "gamification" to engage a growing army of users (300 million and counting). (Gamification is the innovative use of traditional gaming functionality in non-game applications.) Dunaway has had an exceptional career building tech companies, including serving as chief marketing officer of Yahoo! (the company's emphasis, not ours). She reveals her commitment to empowerment leadership in untold ways, including the language of her "personal operating guide," playfully titled "There's Something about Cammie," which she shares with colleagues. In it, she includes her decades-old personal mission: "Be a positive influence on the lives of people around me. Encourage them, challenge them, help them to fulfill their potential."

b. The name "1844" is a reference to the year that the first black man, Macon Bolling Allen, was admitted to practice law in America.

Duolingo has achieved a striking 50:50 gender ratio for new software engineers at the company, with an industry-leading 70 percent people of color represented in their most recent class of starting engineers. The company achieved these milestones by making major changes to its recruiting strategy, including refusing to recruit at universities where fewer than 18 percent of women are represented in computer science programs (the national average). Like many leaders working toward inclusion, Dunaway is vocal about the importance of being uncompromising in her hiring criteria, even "when that meant that some jobs stayed open for months." The lesson she takes from her experience is the power of patience and persistence, of *knowing* without a shadow of a doubt that marginalized talent is out there.[3]

We brought the same conviction to our work with WeWork, the coworking company that's still rebuilding as we write this, after a change in leadership and disrupted IPO.[4] Full disclosure: we're still advising the company and on record for being decidedly bullish on its prospects.[5] We believe in the company, in part, because its commitment to inclusion runs deep. WeWork's passionate, frontline community teams are devoted to inclusive hiring. Whenever they interact with senior leadership, suggestions pour in about how to be more inclusive to working moms, people of color, military veterans, immigrants . . . round it off to everyone. Not surprisingly, in the most recent year-end survey about employee priorities, inclusion topped the list.

Part of our mission at WeWork was to help achieve equal representation of talented women in all parts of the organization. (See the sidebar "How to Attract Great Women.") Women already represented 50 percent of the workforce, but those numbers weren't being reflected at the top, at least not consistently. As part of this work, we invested time in recruiting women we *didn't already know*. One lesson from this effort is that even after a long, rigorous recruiting

How to Attract Great Women

We often get asked for our advice on how to recruit more women, in response to our unabashed skepticism when companies lament, "We can't find any!" Here is a summary of what we've learned:

Look fearlessly at your current practices. If your existing recruiting processes reliably produce employees of the male but not female varieties (much less anyone in between), start by acknowledging that you've created a protocol that only succeeds in producing a narrow demographic of employees. Once you've internalized this, then you're ready to design different processes for attracting women.[6]

Be patient. It can take longer to find great women, since most recruiting processes are not optimized for them. In the experience of Jamie Hoobanoff, founder and CEO of the successful search firm The Leadership Agency, if a typical company spends four weeks on a leadership search, there's an 80 percent chance the pipeline will be exclusively male. Extend the search to six or eight weeks, and that number drops to 60 percent. According to Hoobanoff, if you want to recruit more women, then you have to be prepared to spend more time "connecting and convincing."[7]

Find out where the good women are. Odds are they're working hard at their jobs and are happy enough doing so. They likely haven't reached out to a headhunter for help and have turned down overtures from recruiters in the past. If you don't know where concentrations of great women in your field are, then ask the great women you do know. They'll tell you the events they attend, the media they consume, and the people they consider role models.

Do the outreach yourself. Once you've identified a woman you want, do not ask a third-party intermediary to bring them to you, as your agents are far more likely to be brushed off. Recruiters can certainly be part of your support team, but consider making the first move yourself. Keep screening steps to a minimum, and if you must rely on an agent for outreach, make sure their bedside manner is impeccable. One reason then presidential candidate Mitt Romney's "binders of women" comment hit a nerve among professional women was because we know what it feels like to end up in those binders, compiled by someone trying to hit the boss's quota.

Send very clear signals. Once the courtship begins, be clear about your intentions. Don't start the conversation and then say, "We'll get back to you in a few weeks." Don't get close to a deal and then ask for a break to evaluate other candidates. Women receive mixed signals in every part of their lives (Be fearless but vulnerable! Tough but accessible!). If your own signaling gets muddled, then you risk being lumped in with everyone else who has underestimated your candidate or feels ambivalent about powerful women.

Make an offer that does not require negotiation. A tech startup we know successfully recruited an incredible COO by telling her, "We just hired a best-in-class CFO, and he has the best compensation package at the firm. We want to offer you that same package." That's how it's done, people. The signal of value couldn't be clearer, and she doesn't have to worry that she's getting paid less than her male peers for doing equivalent work.

(continued)

Celebrate her leadership ability. Women know you want us for our functional skill set. The best female leaders are where they are because they're very good at fulfilling their job requirements. We are more likely to say yes if—in addition to our practical skills—you make it clear that you value our ability to inspire, empower, and unleash potential.

Assume she has a context. Again, recruit her in context. If a trailing spouse needs a job, use all your resources to help identify opportunities outside your firm. If your candidate is a mom, help her find the right school for her kids. If her aging parents need support, provide the flexibility she may need to quarterback their care. We've found that recruiting a woman in her full context beats competitive offers far more frequently than compensation alone.

Invite her to identify other great women. It doesn't feel great to be the only woman on a senior team, and to have another woman in the room is only a little bit better. Once there are at least three women at the table, however, women are much more likely to contribute freely without feeling the added burden of having to represent all women.[8] If you're not already there, then ask the women you're recruiting for names of other great women

process, getting all the way to the finish line isn't a given for the category of women-you-don't-know. The companies that get this right spend as much energy attracting women as getting them all the way to yes, two very different skill sets.

For example, most senior women have a *context*. They need to live in a certain geography. Or work from home once a week. Or start in the field with whom they'd like to work. In addition to signaling your commitment to building an inclusive leadership team, you'll continue the recruiting momentum. Again, great women tend to know where other great women are.

Ask her for her "indignities" list. These are the practices that create unintended professional stress for many women, things like scheduling important meetings before daycare opens. Identify things you can do to reduce the impact and frequency of these stressors. One favorite example is when companies cover the cost of a babysitter to travel with a breastfeeding mom, allowing her to bring the baby along—in addition to more bonding time, your prized employee gets to avoid the indignity of pumping in an airport bathroom stall and explaining her bottles of breast milk to a TSA agent. An analog for African American men, which Ursula Burns, former CEO of Xerox, has talked about publicly, is making sure there's a local barber in town who knows what to do with black hair.[9]

Make it clear how much you want her. Communicate how excited the company is for your candidate to join the team—and how hard you will work to set her up to succeed wildly. Then follow through completely on that commitment.

their day after they drop their kids off at school. In our case, we have a child with special medical needs and need to live close to a hospital for access to emergency medical care. WeWork explicitly recruited women in the context of their whole lives, which made a big difference in its "yes" yield. By the end of 2019, more than 50 percent of senior roles in the function that piloted a new approach were filled by great women, none of whom had a previous relationship with the company.[10]

Selection means the ability to choose the best employee from a slate of qualified candidates. The more objective your selection criteria, the better off you'll be on the inclusion front. Be wary of squishy, subjective standards such as "best athlete" and "cultural fit," which live almost entirely in the eyes of overconfident beholders. (If you insist on using these kinds of criteria, we advise keeping the process honest by collecting data on prior predictions and then adjusting your confidence as appropriate.) Recognize our very human propensity to have preferences that may diverge from the company's best interest, and save us from ourselves with dispassionate selection guidelines. Define the selection bar as clearly as you can, and then—like Cammie Dunaway—refuse to lower it.[c]

Also think about ways to level the playing field for outsiders. When Samantha Bee launched her late-night comedy series, it was a strategic, creative, and personal priority to build an inclusive writing team. This was a nontrivial undertaking. "It actually takes a lot of effort to change things," Bee said. "It's an ongoing process, and it has to just be a part of your mental state."[11] To increase their chance of success, show runner Jo Miller used a blind submissions process for hiring new writers, stripping names and backgrounds from the material she reviewed.[d] Miller also created an application package that made it clear what submissions should look like, including

c. We often encounter anxiety about lowering the bar in order to achieve better diversity optics. This is often a valid fear of the cynicism that can infect a culture when selection becomes politicized in *any* way. The correction to these concerns is inclusive recruitment processes and rigorous, transparent selection criteria that everyone understands.

d. Software tools such as Blendoor have automated the reduction of hiring bias through functionality that includes anonymization of candidate profiles. Blendoor is now being used by recruiters at Facebook, Google, Twitter, and Airbnb, among other high-influence firms.

guidance on insider lingo and formatting. These changes—along with the relentless commitment to change things—helped the show create a writers' room with a 50:50 gender ratio, unprecedented for late-night television.[12]

Whatever you decide to do, build accountability into the process. WeWork created an analytic tool that identified where the diversity metrics shifted in its hiring processes. In addition to the demographics of who was being hired, we could also see the profiles of who was screened out, who was brought in for a live interview, who made it to the final interview stage, and so on. At every step in the process, we gained visibility into decision trends. In a healthy process, demographic proportions remain fairly consistent from one stage to another. In a process that needs attention, proportions shift along the way. This shift can be explained in any number of ways, for example, by a hiring manager who is less familiar with the gaps in experience that a working mom might have. The tool gave leadership the data to educate managers and make targeted changes.

The point is to develop and use metrics that advance the cause of inclusion—and to avoid the fate of "balanced slates." Sometime in the last ten to twenty years, organizations started adopting policies requiring diverse candidate slates. The practice gained visibility in 2003, when the NFL required teams with a head coaching vacancy to interview one or more candidates of color. Called the "Rooney Rule" after Dan Rooney, former owner of the Pittsburgh Steelers and chair of the NFL's diversity committee, the league famously declared that the way to make sure that there are more black coaches was to ensure that black candidates were interviewed for every head coaching position.

Here's the problem: when the Rooney rule was implemented in 2003, there were three black head coaches in the NFL.[13] And in 2019, sixteen years after the policy had been widely adopted throughout the league as the diversity gold standard, there were three black head coaches in the NFL. Our take on balanced slates—and every other policy designed to promote diversity and inclusion—is that if they work to help you achieve your goals, then you should use them. And if they don't work, for whatever reason, then you should scrap them and try something else. Policies are only as good as their outcomes.

Which brings us to hiring quotas. Quotas tend to be blunt-force interventions of last resort that can help to deliver better diversity numbers, but they don't help much with the underlying drivers of belonging and inclusion. They don't help you with the challenges of setting up a diverse group of people to thrive and can breed cynicism, resentment, and insecurity along the way. And yet. Sometimes quotas are necessary to make progress toward a more equitable world when other approaches have failed.[e]

Step two: Make sure everyone has an equal opportunity to thrive

In our experience, the opportunity to thrive has two practical drivers: a *culture* that values inclusion and widespread access to *development* opportunities. Later in the book, we'll spend more time on the mechanics of culture, but we also want to highlight the role of culture here, given how central it is to the experience of belonging inside organizations.

A culture of inclusion has four levels: safe, welcome, celebrated, and cherished. These levels can be visualized in our "inclusion dial" in figure 4-1. We often draw people into this discussion by asking them to measure the inclusiveness of their teams using this tool.

e. See histories of the civil rights movements in the United States and South Africa for the compelling case for quotas as a necessary but insufficient response to systematic discrimination.

FIGURE 4-1

The inclusion dial

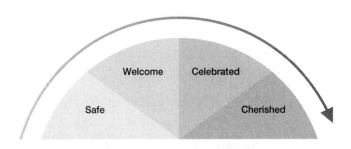

The definitions we use for each of these progressive stages are:

1. *Safe.* Employees feel physically and emotionally safe in the workplace, regardless of who they are.

2. *Welcome.* Employees feel welcome in the workplace, regardless of who they are; they can bring their "whole selves" to work without penalty.

3. *Celebrated.* Employees feel celebrated in the workplace *because of* who they are; they are rewarded for contributing their unique ideas and perspectives.

4. *Cherished.* A culture of inclusion permeates the organization; leaders embrace differences among employees as a source of competitive advantage, and there is minimal variability in the experience of belonging across individuals, teams, and functions.

Where on the dial would you locate your team? Keep in mind that not everyone in a group may experience the same stages at the same times. There may be trends in who feels safe versus welcome versus celebrated (or none of the above), patterns that can become road maps to the inclusion work that needs to be done. In addition, as one person or profile moves up the dial, an unintended effect may be that other people and profiles move down. For example, as some cultures have become more inclusive of women, some men in those same cultures have become more afraid of the costs of inadvertently doing or saying the wrong things. If this is the case on your team, we urge empathy and direct dialogue. Sustainable solutions to inclusion must make *everyone* better off.

Let's explore these definitions in more detail. As a foundation, everyone must feel *safe* when they come to work. Full stop. And leaders must protect and empower those employees who are more likely to experience the *absence* of safety. One classic expression of this vulnerability is the reality that your female employees have a higher risk of being sexually harassed, and this risk alone can impact mental and even physical health.[14] In response, companies need good policies for preventing and addressing misconduct, reinforced by a culture that refuses to tolerate it.[15] If you can't provide a baseline of physical and emotional security for people, then don't bother focusing on the next three levels. You're unlikely to make much progress.

Once you can confidently check the safety box, you can start working on the next challenge: making sure that everyone feels *welcome* in the workplace, including those who represent difference. That difference could be highly visible—black employees in a largely white environment—or less visible identities such as religion, political affiliation, or sexual orientation. It could mean being a single, thirty-something parent on a team populated by twenty-somethings with no problem attending frequent late-night meetings. It could also mean scraping together sick days and time for medical appointments for someone battling a "hidden" disability like MS.

Colleagues who deviate from the majority profile in some way should feel as if they can still bring their whole selves to work without penalty. They should feel as if they have the right to take up just as much space as the people around them. This is also where the idea of *psychological safety* lives, a concept developed by our colleague and friend Amy Edmondson to describe cultures where—among other things that are essential to high-performing teams—"people are comfortable being themselves."[16]

Once people feel safe and welcome, regardless of their differences, the next milestone in a culture of inclusion is to be valued and celebrated *because of* our differences. A culture that celebrates difference assumes that difference is a limitless source of creativity, innovation, and organizational strength. We believe that Salesforce is one such culture, and the company's chief equality officer, Tony Prophet, is a persuasive messenger for the profound implications for both employees and organizations.

In explaining his unconventional title ("chief diversity officer" remains the industry norm), Prophet emphasized that diversity is the starting place, but it's not enough. The real magic, he argues, happens when "you feel seen, you feel included, you feel *valued*." That experience, in Prophet's view, becomes a competitive asset that's analogous to a mosaic, with distinct and complex pieces coming together to make a more magnificent whole: "[T]he result is the beauty and the melding of ideas."[17]

The final frontier in a culture of inclusion is for the celebration of difference to become so ingrained institutionally that employees feel *cherished* for their uniqueness and experience minimal variability across individuals, teams, and functions. This is the point of no return in the campaign for belonging. It's the point at which we no longer feel lucky to have an inclusive manager, the point at which we're all taking exquisite care of people who are different from us with unshakable confidence that their difference makes us better.

This is a primary focus for Michel Doukeris, CEO of Anheuser-Busch. He is passionate in his belief that "inclusion drives diversity, not the other way around" and is championing efforts to create a culture of belonging in every corner of the company. Doukeris believes that if Anheuser-Busch can get all the way to "cherished" on the inclusion dial, then he will be able to unleash the full potential of the organization. "Our greatest strength is our people," he told us. "If we get this right, we will be unstoppable."

The inclusive meeting

What does the progression of the inclusion dial look like in practice? Let's use a routine team meeting as an illustrative example. Imagine that you're a young black or brown woman on a primarily white team. The meeting is scheduled, and you feel *safe* showing up. The guy who had been repeatedly asking you out via the company's Slack channel, despite you asking him to stop, has been removed from your team.

You walk in and a white colleague makes you feel *welcome* by inviting you to sit next to her. The team lead—an older man—opens by saying, "I'd like to get the team's advice, and I want to hear from everyone." You're feeling pretty good at this point, comfortable and ready to participate.

The meeting continues, and there seems to be convergence in what the group thinks the plan should be. (Note that this is the point at which most organizations declare victory and move forward with an idea.) You have a different idea, but you don't want to rock the boat or hold the team back. Then the team lead says, "OK, if we were to think about this problem *differently,* what would that look like?" A few new voices jump into the discussion. The team lead says, "Excellent! I never would have thought of that!" to ensure these voices are *celebrated* for making the group's thinking more rigorous.

He then says, "What else are we missing?" His response shifts the dynamics in the room, and you decide to share your idea. Your colleagues respectfully debate your idea; they identify some risks that you hadn't thought about before, but people seem energized by the ambition of it. The lead says, "Listen, it might not work, but I love the audacity of [insert your name]'s idea. It's the kind of thinking we need to win." You leave the meeting feeling *cherished* by the company for your ability to think differently—and without any doubts that you belonged in the room. This feeling has become familiar to you. You felt the same way in a different meeting, led by a different manager, last week. (See the sidebar "How to Create Spaces Where Queer People Feel Like They Belong.")

Development is the deliberate investment in the growth and evolution of the people around you. Development can be both formal (e.g., training programs and corporate universities) and informal (e.g., mentoring and access to stretch assignments). As we've revealed at this point, we believe passionately in the value of both types, and we're convinced that people can grow at lightning speed with the right kind of developmental investment.

Some leaders resist the concept of development, preferring a "sink or swim" approach rooted in the following logic: hire as well as you can, make the job requirements clear, largely leave people alone to figure out how to thrive, and may the best people win. The idea here is that a healthy meritocracy is a substitute for development, with the added kicker of helping you sort the strong from the weak.

This approach may seem reasonable on the surface, but it tends to get wobbly in execution. One reason is that *informal* development is happening all of the time, whether or not you code it as such. And it is rarely distributed fairly: some of your best "swimmers" have easy access to it, while other people, as a colleague of ours recently characterized, are experiencing a daily ice-bucket challenge. What's worse, we often throw people who are different from us into the deep end, without realizing how much informal scaffolding we're

How to Create Spaces Where Queer People Feel Like They Belong

Here's the thing: the future is queer, arguably very queer.* By some measures, less than half of your future workforce will identify as heterosexual, and more than a third won't view gender as an essential, immutable characteristic.[18] Here is a brief, practical summary for how to prepare for this future and create professional spaces that are inclusive of queer identities:

1. **Assume nothing.** An LGBT+ person is not always visible, and your powers of observation may not be as reliable as you think. That gorgeous woman in operations (and kick-ass Manolos) may have been assigned a different gender at birth, and that buttoned-up guy in finance may be going home every night to his equally buttoned-up husband.

2. **Get comfortable with fluidity.** As human beings, we are pattern-seeking, categorizing machines. When we can't find a label or frame of reference, we can quickly get uncomfortable. Know that we were wired that way a long time ago, for survival in a world where ambiguity was dangerous, and do what you can to *relax* about this one.

3. **Get educated.** There are so many great advocates and organizations working to teach people about the complexities of queerness in the workplace, including the differences between gender identity and sexual preference (and what to do with that ever-evolving, phonetically awkward LGBT+ acronym). Organizations that can help you get started include GLAAD, the Human Rights Campaign, and Stonewall. Accept their generous, accessible offers to meet you wherever you are on your exposure to LGBT+ issues.

4. **Ask for pronouns.** Does your new colleague use he, she, or they? In some industries and geographies, there's a growing trend to declare your pronouns in your email signature (as in, "Betty Rubble, Pronouns: she/her"). Including this information normalizes conversations about pronouns and sets a precedent for respecting all gender identities. At the very least, get comfortable with the idea that a person's pronouns may not be what you'd expect.

5. **Respect people's privacy.** Queer people can end up on the receiving end of a barrage of questions about their histories. While engaging in this way can promote understanding and mutual respect, please be on your very best behavior. Questions like "What's your real name?" or any variation on "What's going on below the belt?" are offensive. Before proceeding, ask yourself if you need to know the answer to treat this person with respect.

6. **Build private bathrooms.** We can't overstate how fraught and exposing it is to navigate public bathrooms when you don't fit cleanly into the world's definition of the gender icon on the door. It forces you to confront your difference multiple times a day, in the stares and comments of your fellow bathroom patrons. This type of exchange isn't limited to bathrooms, but to endure it in a shared, intimate space that's unmonitored and away from the herd amplifies the discomfort. It's not always financially possible to go private, but if it's feasible, we strongly encourage it.

(continued)

7. **Remember that family may be complicated. Or not.** There's no typical queer family structure or context. There may be kids in the picture. Or not. If there are kids, don't assume you know how those kids were conceived. There may be estranged parents. Or wildly supportive, PFLAG-chapter-starting parents. There may or may not be a serious partner in the mix. If there is a serious partner, they may or may not be married. Also, their loved ones may not be formally related to them, as the idea of "chosen family" is much more prevalent in queer communities.

8. **Proactively support your queer employees.** This can be expressed in lots of different ways, from putting up that rainbow flag (we notice all of them) to supporting a queer employee resource group. We particularly like The Safe Zone Project's (free!) curriculum for workplace inclusivity training, complete with a sticker you can put up as a reminder of your commitment to ensuring that LGBT+ employees can bring who they are to work.[19]

giving to people who are like us, in ways we sometimes don't recognize as developmental, such as a casual conversation at the preschool fundraiser. Even if you believe in sink or swim—and to be clear, we emphatically don't—it's important to make sure that informal practices aren't disadvantaging some.

What does informal development look like? It might be selecting who gets the special project with access to important clients, or who gets to participate on strategic site visits with senior leaders.

9. **Champion the visibility of queer leaders.** Make it clear that queer people can thrive at your organization, and encourage your willing, high-status LGBT+ colleagues to be visible. Deirdre O'Brien, senior vice president of people and retail at Apple, describes coming out in the 1990s as one of her toughest—and proudest—professional decisions. "I was scared, but knew I had to bring my full self to Apple," she said. In her current role, she describes it as a "responsibility and a privilege to show up every day in support of our underrepresented team members."[20]

10. **Listen.** Ask your LGBT+ colleagues what you can do to help create spaces where queer people feel safe, welcome, celebrated, and cherished. Show up for the conversation with that magic mix of openness and humility.

*Note that we use the terms "queer" and "LGBT+" interchangeably, both in this book and in our own conversations.

These opportunities are rarely distributed thoughtfully when we rely on them happening organically, and so we should stop relying on them happening organically. Instead, make access to informal development as deliberate and systematic as you can. Train people on how to do it well—both how to develop others and how to get the support and input you need to succeed—and find ways to keep yourself honest on how well it's going for *everyone* on the team.

Which brings us back to *formal* development. Informal development can go a long way, but often not far enough, particularly for high-growth organizations. Again, one of the lessons of working with Uber is that when organizations are moving at a rapid speed, there's rarely enough time and space for sufficient informal support and mentorship, particularly for managers. Early-stage companies run an added risk of underinvesting in an HR skill set, which means they sometimes don't know what they don't know in terms of the value and mechanics of people development. Formal development programs can help address these dynamics, and increasingly there are ways to do it without breaking the bank or distracting people from their day jobs.

Step three: Promote your best people using a rigorous, transparent system

A promotions process is working when decisions about whether to promote someone are self-evident. Among other things, this requires full transparency in promotions criteria, for both candidates and gatekeepers. Everyone should know exactly what it takes to get to the next level.

The absence of that clarity comes at a big price. It creates space for subjectivity in promotions decisions, with all its potential downside, including the alienation and frustration of talented people who are more likely to get overlooked. It also takes up outsized space in the organization's emotional life. As achievement-oriented creatures, many of your best people are thinking about promotion, some of them *all the time*, and making us guess at what it will take is not in the company's best interest. You're also making the women and people of color, in particular, suspicious of bespoke processes that can be influenced by who you know and how well you know them, since we're often on the losing side of that proposition. To avoid this scenario, make the objective drivers of advancement clear, sharing the news far and wide.

In addition, chase down any uncomfortable demographic patterns in who's getting promoted. Note that the data you need are sometimes held under lock and key by well-meaning protectors of the institution. Protectors play an essential role, but they can also unintentionally get in the way of progress. Handle the data safely and kindly, but also with the resolve to improve.

It's essential to approach these questions with the humility that your own theory of the case may be wrong. When we started working on issues of gender equity at Harvard Business School, male faculty members were being promoted at twice the rate of female faculty members. As we talked to our senior colleagues about how to explain this phenomenon, two prevailing hypotheses emerged: either the school was making biased decisions systematically or men are better prepared than women to be promoted.

We put aside our own point of view and did an investigation into which hypothesis was right. We looked at fifteen years of résumés (that's how long we had been at the school, so we knew the candidates) and found true variance related to gender: men who were up for promotion had, on average, a higher number of top-tier publications than their female peers. And then we pushed further, channeling the famous "five whys" of root cause analysis. Why did the magnificent female scholars in our community tend to have fewer publications? Why were these talented women less productive academically?

We found a trend that surprised us: overall, women were holding on to draft manuscripts for extended periods of time—often for a year or more—before submitting them for publication. And while they were polishing their work toward an relentless goal of perfection, their male counterparts were submitting works in progress early and often, getting critical feedback on their ideas and shortening the timeline to a publication's ultimate acceptance. They weren't letting perfectionism get in the way of participating in the industry's cycle of feedback and improvement.

We began a campaign to encourage women to send their papers out sooner, even if they weren't yet "perfect," and we quickly began to see equal numbers of papers published by men and women. Once we determined an accurate causal context, we were able to tackle the right problem. If instead we had assumed that bias was the root cause and, for example, mandated implicit bias training for all faculty members, we would have missed the mark (and potentially stoked the confusion and resentment of the community). (See the sidebar "Why We're Often Skeptical of 360-Degree Reviews.")

Another opportunity you have is to build your commitment to inclusion—and to empowerment leadership more broadly—directly into your promotions criteria. That's what Kathleen Hogan, chief people officer at Microsoft, did when she joined CEO Satya Nadella in shepherding one of the most exciting corporate turnarounds in a generation (more on this story in our culture chapter).

When Hogan joined the executive team, promotions were largely based on individual impact. By the time the company's performance-review system was done being overhauled, individual impact still mattered, but just as important was how much someone contributed to *other people's* success. As a rebounding Microsoft went on to embrace inclusion as one of its three cannot-get-it-wrong priorities, Hogan made it a key criterion in all performance evaluations.[21] These changes reflected Nadella and his team's full-bodied commitment to inclusion, but also an important difference in the mentality of leaders who get this right: they see creating equal access to the experience of belonging as indistinguishable from their broader leadership mandate.

Why We're Often Skeptical of
360-Degree Reviews

A few years ago, we spent some time with a government agency that was struggling with an uncomfortable fact pattern: the agency was succeeding in recruiting great women, but these women were not getting promoted beyond a certain level. At some point, talented women were systematically getting stuck, and no one could figure out why.

In situations like this, we had learned to start with a single question: Do you use 360-degree reviews or other evaluation tools that incorporate anonymous observations? In our experience of seeing the ubiquitous, well-intentioned 360 review play out in practice, people tended to respond differently to men and women, particularly when a woman held formal power. In reviews of male and female managers of equal caliber, women were regularly, well, skewered, while their male peers were often left unscathed and even celebrated, sometimes for the very same behaviors.

The short explanation for this pattern is that people are more likely to say, well, dopey things about women, particularly when they have the chance to do so anonymously (see internet). A case experiment famously asked MBA students to evaluate the profiles of Heidi Roizen, a Silicon Valley entrepreneur known for her assertive style, and her male alter ego, "Howard."[22] The case asked, "Should your VC firm hire this candidate?" Some classes received Heidi's profile, others received Howard's. Apart from the name and gender of the protagonists, the profiles were identical, containing descriptors like "aggressive," "independent," and a "captain of industry." Overall, students rated Howard significantly more favorably than Heidi. Traits

(continued)

that made Howard appear competent and desirable, it seems, made Heidi unlikable and a risky bet.

We're going to skip the explanatory part of this discussion—the part about the gender baggage we're all dragging around—and simply advise using anonymous evaluation tools sparingly, or at least with the recognition that they don't reliably bring out the best in us. If you must invite everyone to opine on each other's strengths and weaknesses, then we suggest first training people in how to perform productive, unbiased evaluations. Figuring out how to separate signal from noise from ego in assessing our colleagues is varsity stuff, and we shouldn't just be throwing people into the deep end with it, which most 360 processes effectively do. (Another way to mediate this risk is to involve a skilled facilitator in data collection and analysis, someone who can provide the context and filtering themselves.)

Also consider making the feedback we give others part of *our own* evaluation. If someone rates everyone the same, then they're not doing a good job. If the differences are arbitrary or retaliatory, then they're not doing a good job. And if their ratings are thoughtful, evidence-based, self-aware, and sensitive to institutional context, then they should be celebrated for their contributions (and probably promoted). Our point is that evaluation is a skill and we should honor it as such—and not *dishonor* it by subjecting each other to our unfiltered, anonymous reactions.

The other pattern we see in 360s is that something completely new almost always pops up—again, particularly for women. A curveball comes out of nowhere, some transgression she's never heard about before, from a source she's unable to identify, at a stage in the process where it's hard for her to provide context or defend herself. This violates everything we know about how constructive advice is best given and received (see chapter 3). To review, for constructive advice to be productive, it must be layered on top of a foundation of trust. Anonymity, by definition, obscures that foundation and eliminates accountability for the saying of dopey things, increasing the chance that the feedback will do more harm than good.

Getting back to our government agency, it was indeed subjecting everyone to extensive 360 reviews and relying heavily on them for promotions decisions. As an experiment, we asked the senior leaders to develop a list of equivalent performers with equivalent reputations—men and women who they were confident the organization perceived similarly. We then asked the leaders to study the corresponding 360s and observe what was written about these employees.

The leaders came back stunned—it was Heidi and Howard all over again. They agreed that if an outsider had read these evaluations without context or personal experience with the candidates, they would in no way conclude there was equivalence. And outsiders *were* reading them, since promotions often meant being transferred to another part of the organization. As a result of the experiment, the team decided to eliminate anonymity in its evaluation process and bring feedback out of the shadows.

We invite you to do the same.

Step four: Retain, retain, retain

Once you've hired, developed, and promoted great people of all varieties, you now have to *retain* them. In today's talent marketplace, this is often a significant challenge.

The solution? *Earn* the right to keep your people, every single day. We recommend you start (stay with us here) by making lots of paranoid assumptions. Assume your competitors are looking at your inclusive, well-oiled talent machine as their own development pipeline. Assume your best people are getting calls from enthusiastic headhunters on a weekly, even daily, basis. (In our experience, African-American software engineers get called by recruiters at an average rate of *every day*.) Assume a few of them are feeling restless and/or some subset of the following: underchallenged, undervalued, underpaid, and underappreciated. Assume that someone put a great offer in front of them today, and they're talking to their loved ones right now about the pros and cons of making the jump.

Wake up every morning with a commitment to create the conditions where your employees aren't even tempted to take that first call. That process is going to look different for every organization, but it always starts with open-hearted, open-minded inquiry into what's getting in the way of *everyone* thriving, particularly the ones who are contributing the most. One of the things we like to do when we start working with companies is to sit down one-on-one with senior women and people of color and ask, "What does this organization need to do to keep awesome people like you?"

The answers often surprise company leadership. One straightforward challenge we see is the burdening of marginalized groups with a "representation tax" on their workload. Asking the same group of people to sit on hiring committees and be visible when important stakeholders are in town can backfire if it means they're doing significantly more uncredited work than their colleagues. As our friend Bozoma Saint John, chief marketing officer at Endeavor, has asked, "Why do I, as a black woman, have to fix it all? There's way more of you than there are of me. We need some help out here."

Also keep in mind that just because someone has "made it," so to speak, it doesn't mean that slights and indignities have been eliminated from their daily experience. Status doesn't inoculate your colleagues from the pain of other people's biases and ignorance, or from the scars they may have earned crashing through glass ceilings. Promotion doesn't heal all wounds. Your work is not done when you give someone a corner office and a bottle of champagne.

So go ahead: be proactive and execute steps one through three with excellence and joy. Attract great people, give them interesting work to do, and invest in them as if your company's future depends on it. If they deserve a promotion, give it to them in a timely manner. Don't make them wait. Don't make them go to a competitor in order to get the role, title, and compensation package they already earned on your watch.

And in the name of all that is right and just in the world, pay them fairly for the work they do. One of the most infuriating parts of working while female is to discover that our male peers are getting paid more than we are for equal work. In tech, in particular, we often saw awesome, hard-working women demoralized when they learned that junior men on their teams were being paid more than they were. We're seeing this anger play out on the cultural mainstage right now in the debate over equal pay for professional soccer players in the United States. In March 2019, the US Women's National Team sued the US Soccer Federation (USSF) for gender discrimination, alleging that they are paid less and given less support than the men's team, despite performing better on key metrics such as title wins and league revenue.[23]

It's a fight the USSF is destined to lose, thanks in part to the determined advocacy of star players like Megan Rapinoe, who has captured hearts and minds on this issue and channeled support for the team into effective change making. When Rapinoe and her teammates delivered yet another World Cup title in 2019 (their fourth), it was no accident that the stadium erupted into chants of "Equal pay! Equal Pay!"

The bottom line is this: don't make women work so hard to simply get what they deserve. Pay people equally for doing the same work, regardless of gender identity or any other distinguishing characteristic. And when they go above and beyond, reward them accordingly.

Truth and reconciliation

Most inclusion journeys involve some reckoning with an organization's past, where justice for historical missteps and transgressions fits into the fight for a better future. In January 2014, Dean Nitin Nohria apologized for Harvard Business School's historical treatment of women in extraordinary remarks to a packed room of alumni. We did not have the privilege of being there, but according to reports, no one in the audience dared to even breathe as Nohria acknowledged that HBS women had felt "disrespected, left out, and unloved by the school."[24] "The school owed you better," he declared unequivocally, "and I promise it will be better."

His words rocketed around alumnae networks and meant a lot to us personally. When you are asked to operate in an environment that makes you feel less than fully seen, included, or valued—Tony Prophet's lovely triad—a part of you feels a bit crazy, unsure of what's real and what's not, in addition to the other negative emotions you're trying not to normalize. To have that experience described as unacceptable can be a powerfully grounding and restorative act.

When people ask us how an organization can heal from a painful past, we often reflect on Nohria's courageous remarks. In our experience, leaders need to confront their organization's history with both optimism and honesty. Optimism is about building a better tomorrow, fixing an organization's problems with the kind of humility and resourcefulness we explore throughout this book. Honesty is about taking radical responsibility for the things that went wrong and the human costs of those mistakes.

In most organizations, honesty also includes some process of holding individuals accountable for their actions and/or inactions. We often say that organizational change can fix good people behaving badly, but it can't fix "bad" people behaving badly, employees with an established pattern of toxicity, discrimination, or misconduct. We believe that your only defensible option for the latter category is to separate those employees from the company. We're not ruling out anyone's rehabilitation, but it doesn't need to happen on your watch if there's been a high personal and cultural price for someone's behavior. The cost of dehumanizing others—at a minimum—must be giving up the privilege of being around them. Of course, determining who's in this camp requires a good, fair, transparent process, as well as institutional confidence in the outcomes of that process. Pitchfork justice helps nobody.

We also want to say, for the record, that we believe forgiveness and redemption are legitimate options in many situations. In our experience, giving people the space to mess up and learn from their mistakes can have an extraordinary impact on organizations. This kind of grace can unleash powerful new forces into a company's ecosystem, including deep humility and an infectious commitment to do better. Notably, it's in these environments where we've seen the fastest progress toward true belonging and the most profound healing along the way. (See the sidebar "Finding Grace at Riot Games.")

Finding Grace at Riot Games

In chapter 6, we'll talk more about Riot Games's work to reconcile with its past as a fast-moving startup that struggled to fully embrace difference. Under the leadership of CEO Nicolo Laurent, Riot has put inclusion at the very center of both its cultural values and strategic vision. Reflecting on the work the company is doing to get there, Laurent described the evolution in his own thinking on the relationship between belonging and scale: "Inclusion isn't something that runs parallel to growth," he told us. "It's *foundational* to it. It's what makes sustainable growth possible."

Laurent exhibits the kind of principled grace we believe is needed to heal organizations. As part of the company's redemption journey, he honored the considerable pain that surfaced—actively soliciting and investigating complaints—and took disciplinary action that included the termination of senior leaders. But Laurent also made space for more nuanced responses. One key decision he made was to support COO Scott Gelb, one of the company's earliest technology leaders, even as Gelb was very publicly criticized for allegations that he engaged in unprofessional humor with his male colleagues, particularly during Riot's early days, which had the unintended effect of creating a less inclusive environment.

Although the company's policy was not to speak publicly about specific cases, Laurent made an exception for Gelb, given Gelb's role on the leadership team and in response to false rumors circulating about him. After an outside law firm and special committee of the board reviewed Gelb's case, he was asked to take a two-month, unpaid leave and undergo sensitivity training. As Gelb prepared to take his leave, Laurent sent a companywide email that highlighted Gelb's commitment to make Riot a place where everyone had a chance to thrive. In closing, he wrote, "I will root for him, will support him through this journey, and I will leverage him as a great leader when he returns . . . I hope you will join me."

The reality of Gelb's story was not always what it appeared to be, at least not on the surface. Gelb had an established track record of building and leading diverse teams—both at Riot and in previous roles—and had been a behind-the-scenes champion of inclusion at the company. He had a heightened sensitivity to the experience of being an outsider, which he earned growing up "as a short, scrawny Jewish kid in the Midwest . . . a geek bullied for loving computers and video games in the eighties, when everyone thought they were a waste of time." And *yet*, Gelb is the first to point out that these things didn't translate into a deep enough awareness of Riot's culture challenges or the role he might have played in them. He told us, "One of the most impactful experiences of my life was hearing directly from Rioters that we were letting them down on inclusion. I knew we had work to do, but I didn't know how much."

Over the next twelve months, Gelb worked on his development as a leader, taking a clear-eyed look at his own patterns and choices. Specifically, he worked on how to *consistently* be a more inclusive and authentic leader. A year later, Gelb is thriving at Riot, skillfully executing his mandate to expand the company's games portfolio. He has also become one of Riot's most effective leaders in advancing the company's inclusion agenda. Angela Roseboro, Riot's new chief diversity officer, names Gelb as one of her most committed allies in her work to make Riot an industry-leading model for belonging.

(continued)

An important plot point in Gelb's story is that Laurent and other Rioters stood by him at critical moments in the process. Several colleagues, including a number of senior women Gelb had mentored or managed, publicly cited him as a supportive leader and unwavering advocate for their professional growth. Others stopped him quietly in a hallway or after a meeting to apologize for making unfair assumptions about him. These moments are Gelb's most vivid and emotional memories of the last year, and they fuel his resolve to help make Riot a place where inclusion is cherished. This future is within reach, in part, because Rioters created an opening for shared humanity, vulnerability, and growth, both their own and Gelb's. Another word for this choice is *grace*.

Black working moms

When we began this work, the shorthand we offered people who wanted to get belonging right was that if you made your organization better for women, then you were likely to make it better for everyone. Over time, we evolved that advice to, "Make it better for black women," to reflect the complexity of carrying around more than one marginalized identity. Sheryl Sandberg recently offered us this variation: "Make it better for black *working moms*." If a black working mom has as good a chance of thriving in your organization as anyone else, then you're getting a whole bunch of things right.

If you discover you have a long way to go before she feels cherished, don't despair. It's easy to feel overwhelmed by the forces working against full inclusion, including the anxiety that many organizations feel right now about getting it wrong in an era when everyone's watching. In our experience, the antidote is to commit, *truly* commit to the idea that inclusion is an urgent, achievable goal. We've learned that there's incredible power in simply moving forward, in bringing some can-do, lesbian spirit to the challenge of universal belonging. If you can replace anxiety and inertia with optimism and progress, few organizations will be able to resist your charm.

And now for the biggest leap in your leadership journey, the one from presence to absence. Belonging is a critical part of your leadership practice, one that—like trust and love—typically requires your presence. We're now going to move on to the chapters on absence and the tools you have to unleash people when being present isn't an option.

Questions for Reflection

- ✓ Who gets to thrive in your organization? Do you see demographic patterns in performance or engagement? What about promotion and retention?

- ✓ How would your company benefit if every single employee felt as if they could show up authentically and contribute their full capacity?

- ✓ Which of these words describes the way underrepresented people feel as employees of your organization: *safe, welcome, celebrated, cherished*? Which actions can you take right now to move your team along the inclusion dial?

- ✓ Whose support, endorsement, and/or participation will you need to achieve your inclusion and belonging goals? Who needs to be convinced that inclusion is an urgent, achievable goal?

- ✓ What is likely to get in the way of advancing your goals? How will you overcome these barriers?

PART TWO

ABSENCE

n the first section of the book, we explored how to empower others as a result of your presence. In this section—the chapters on absence —we move on to the second part of our leadership definition: making sure that impact continues in your absence. From our perspective, this is where the leadership path takes its most interesting turn, where you get to change lives and accelerate action at the scale of organizations (and beyond). It's also the point at which it's *really* not about you. Indeed, you're not even in the room for this part.

Let us explain: up to this point, we've explored how to lead individuals and teams who might as well be in the same room with you, or at least in an office or digital workspace nearby. Trust, love, and belonging are all empowering leadership currencies you exchange directly with other people. When you get it right, we've argued, the performance of your teammates looks something like figure 1-1. Again, your presence progressively unleashes the potential of other people.

But what happens in this model when you leave the proverbial room? In the most common leadership dynamics, when a leader exits—even temporarily—the performance of others plateaus or even drops. On the one hand, this reinforces the leader's value (and ego). On the other hand, it limits their influence to the people they interact with on a regular basis. When you're leading an organization, it turns out, then you're actually somewhere else most of the time, at least from the perspective of your colleagues. Most of your people are making most of their decisions without you. To unleash their potential in your absence will require additional leadership tools.

The good news is that you have two very powerful leadership levers that do not require you to be anywhere near the action. *Strategy* and *culture* are invisible forces that can shape organizations and empower other people—*lots* of other people—whether or not you happen to be present.[a] As a result, the most successful leaders spend a disproportionate amount of time getting strategy and culture right—and broadcasting both to every far-flung corner of the company.

Pulling this off allows you to empower anyone, anywhere in the organization, and change your leadership performance curve from the more typical B or C paths in figure A to an A path, where the performance of others improves even in your absence (think "A" for Absence).

"A" leaders create impact that endures days, years, and even decades after they've left the room. Their people go out into the world without them and thrive, even when they're far away from the mother ship. It's the ultimate measure of empowerment leadership and the focus of our next two chapters.

---

a. Peter Drucker allegedly once said, "Culture eats strategy for breakfast," setting up a debate about which of the two is more powerful. In practice, culture usually wins this showdown, but only because strategy is rarely articulated well enough to influence most employees. Whether we like it or not, culture gets to flamboyantly declare its intentions with a constant flow of informal signals and behavioral cues. Meanwhile, strategy often gets stuck inside the minds of a few top lieutenants or buried inside a strategic plan that gets revisited once a year. Honestly, it's not a fair fight.

FIGURE A

Extended leadership performance curve

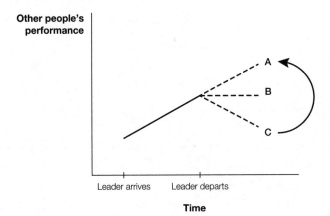

5

STRATEGY

The first frontier of absence leadership is strategy. Strategy, done well, empowers organizations by showing employees how to deploy the resources they control (time, focus, capital, etc.) in the absence of direct, hands-on leadership. This scale of leadership depends on people understanding the strategy well enough to inform their own decisions with it. In our experience, too many companies are held back by strategic confusion below the most senior ranks. Said differently, strategy guides discretionary behavior to the limit of how well you communicate it. This chapter is about removing the artificial limits.

It starts with getting the strategy itself right. In the first part of the chapter, we walk through a framework for designing strategies that delight customers, protect suppliers, and deliver healthy returns to both shareholders and employees. We like the term "value-based" strategy because it focuses on where value is created and captured. But we also reject the idea that strategy is simply a series of technical decisions. We believe that strategy is a direct extension of who you are as a leader. Strategy embeds your own values and beliefs into your organization's behavior. It carries who you are into corners of the company you could never reach on your own. Our challenge to you is to use that superpower to unleash the potential of, well, *everyone*.

What *is* strategy?

At its most basic, strategy describes how an organization wins. The component parts of strategy vary by industry, but the key inputs are typically customers, competitors, and suppliers—the external stake-holders whose decisions can make or break you.[1] We'll reveal up front that we're going to make the controversial choice to put your employees on this list, too. More on that heresy later in the chapter.

Your first job as a strategist is to be better than your competitors at the things that matter most to your customers. This sounds simple enough, but here's the thing: in most cases, this means you'll also have to be *worse* than your competitors at other things, ideally the less important ones. A major lesson of our decade of research on service companies—we wrote a book about this idea—is that organizations that resist and try to be great at everything usually end up in a state of "exhausted mediocrity."[2] Sound familiar?

Here's another way to think about it: one of your central duties as an absent leader is to empower your employees to deploy resources they control without you staring over their shoulders. They could distribute these resources equally, across all potential sources of competitive advantage, but we advise you to help them place those bets more *strategically*. In particular, we suggest underinvesting where it matters least in order to free up the resources to overinvest where it matters most. We propose being bad in the service of great.

A leader who embraced this part of his job was Herb Kelleher, the iconic cofounder and CEO of Southwest Airlines, which remains an exception to the rule that airlines have to lose money and make

FIGURE 5-1

Attribute map for Southwest Airlines (SWA)

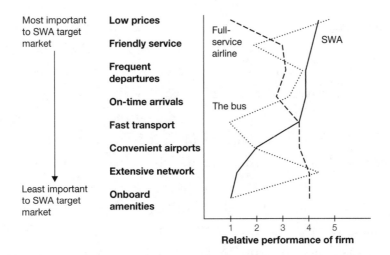

Source: Frances Frei and Anne Morriss, *Uncommon Service: How to Win by Putting Customers at the Core of Your Business* (Harvard Business Review Press, 2012).

their customers sad. On the graph in figure 5-1, the attributes rang-ing from most important to least important for Southwest's target customers are arranged on the vertical axis. For clarity, we call these strategy graphs *attribute maps*.[3] On Southwest's attribute map in figure 5-1, low prices mattered most to Kelleher's target market, with friendly service in the number two spot. At the bottom, an extensive network and onboard amenities mattered least.

Under Kelleher's leadership, Southwest became best-in-class on the attributes that mattered most to its customers *precisely because* it chose to be worst-in-class on the ones that mattered least. The airports Southwest operated out of were in inconvenient locations (for example, its Washington, DC, hub was in Baltimore), but that meant lower costs for the airline, savings it could pass on to price-sensitive customers who were more than willing to give up conve-nience in return for cheaper tickets. Southwest denied passengers any meaningful onboard comforts (including an assigned seat!), which meant it could turn planes around faster at the gate, which meant that the airline got more flying time out of its expensive, airborne assets than its competitors, freeing up even more room to lower prices—the thing its customers wanted most.[4]

These kinds of decisions take real courage, particularly for the leaders among us who do not like to let anyone down. Kelleher once famously received a complaint letter on behalf of an angry grandmother about Southwest's policy of not transferring bags to other airlines.[5] The letter asked for the simple courtesy of transferring her luggage on her way to visit her grandkids. In Kelleher's response—a story he shared far and wide, using it as a teachable moment for the organization—he pointed out that Southwest's business model wouldn't survive if he reversed this policy. If his team had to pause in their turnaround sprints to deal with the complexity and uncertainty of another airline, then Southwest's turnaround advantage would disappear. So Kelleher was very sorry, but he would not be transferring anyone's bags anytime soon.

We love this story, enough to repeat it here, because we can imagine how hard it would have been to say no to this perfectly reasonable woman, making a perfectly reasonable request, representing countless other perfectly reasonable customers frustrated by Southwest's anomalous policies. It would have been strategically excruciating, on one level, to deny her a basic service that every one of the company's cutthroat competitors offered. But in return for this kind of discipline, Kelleher got to build the most successful airline in history.

Dare to be bad: Leader's edition

Whenever we teach people about companies that underachieve on some dimensions in order to excel on others, we get the same question: Does this logic work for people, too? The short answer is *absolutely*. Our male colleagues on the promotions fast track in chapter 4—the ones who were submitting papers before they were perfect—were making this kind of professional trade-off intentionally and *strategically*. They were choosing to deliver lower quality at the beginning of the review process in order to improve faster and produce exceptional results later on. Bad in the service of great. Meanwhile, our female colleagues who were striving for perfection at every stage of the process were more likely to end up with lower output.

The most successful leaders constantly make trade-offs like these, often describing their workdays as relentless exercises in prioritization. They accept that they can only do some things well, and so they choose to do the most important ones. Patty Azzarello became the youngest general manager at HP at thirty-three, ran a billion-dollar software business at thirty-five, and became a CEO at thirty-eight. Reflecting on her exceptional career and the patterns of effective leaders around her, she observed that "the most successful people don't even try to do everything." They apply "ruthless prioritization," in Azzarello's words, while the rest of us become "famous for working hard instead of for doing important things and adding value."[6]

The potential payoff of a dare-to-be-bad mindset can be easiest to envision in a one-on-one relationship. Here's an exercise you can do at your desk: pick a person in your life with whom you want to build a stronger connection. Maybe it's your boss or your partner or even a loved one at home. Consider the following trade-off: What if Super You showed up when it mattered most to them, but it meant that Average You—or even Bummer You—showed up when it mattered least? How would your relationship change as a result? What about your effectiveness or mental health?

Play this out with us on an attribute map. For the person you've selected, rank the activities you share and/or the things you do for

FIGURE 5-2

Sample attribute map

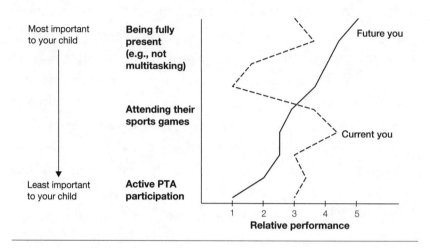

them, from most important to least important. Now give yourself a grade on your current versus optimal performance, some reasonable notion of excellence, 1–5, with 1 being terrible and 5 being outstanding.[a]

Most people end up with a line that looks like the dotted line in figure 5-2. In this example, being fully present in the time you spend with your child is the thing that matters most to them. This means that you're not on the phone when you're at home, not thinking about a work problem in the middle of a conversation about whether Hulk or Superman would win in a matchup, and not secretly checking email in the bathroom when you're supposed to be building Legos. (These are purely hypothetical scenarios used for educational purposes only. Obviously.)

a. We find that most people can do this exercise without gathering more data, but it never hurts to have a direct conversation. Ask your stakeholder some variation of "Of all the things I do, which are most important to you?" This conversation can be a powerful signal of your investment, and the dialogue on its own is often meaningful.

What matters less to this hypothetical child is your regular attendance at PTA meetings. A dare-to-be-bad response to this kind of insight might be to give up the PTA commitment and invest that additional time into making sure you're not bringing work home from the office. Or it might mean redirecting your school volunteering time from PTA events to the sports program, a space where it *is* meaningful for you to be active and visible. Again, the idea here is to be bad, to be downright dreadful, at the things that don't matter in order to be excellent at the things that do. This takes courage and a willingness to give up the fantasy of unlimited capacity. In return, you get to create the space to truly thrive.

Which brings us back to the mission of this book. What we're describing here are the types of personal and professional trade-offs that make great leadership possible. One thing that doesn't get a lot of attention in the leadership discussion is a frank acknowledgment that it takes tremendous energy to do it well. Building trust, maintaining high standards and deep devotion, unleashing the potential of more and varied people: these are nontrivial challenges. If you want to excel at them, do us all a favor and please be bad at something else.

Create (a whole lot) more value than you capture

Once you determine how to create value by strategically winning and losing, it's time to capture some of that value and build a business.[7] Price is the central mechanism that allows you to do that, the knife that divides the value cake between you and your customers. And so your next strategic challenge is to figure out how to price that dare-to-be-bad, attribute-infused, product-service feature bundle you've strategically designed. For simplicity, we're just going to call this your "product."

FIGURE 5-3

Strategic value range

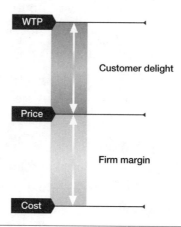

Pricing tends to work better if you understand your customers' maximum willingness to pay (WTP) for a product. In order to attract customers and stay in business, your price should live somewhere between WTP and cost. If your price is higher than WTP, even a penny over, then your customers will walk. If your price is lower than cost, even a penny lower, then you're losing money rather than making it, threatening your existential lifeline as a business.[b] We suggest visualizing your pricing decision on a continuum like the one in figure 5-3.[8] Everything above price but below WTP benefits the customer, so we call this the zone of customer delight. Everything below price but above cost benefits the company in the form of firm margin (the zone of CFO delight).

Where should you draw your price line? This decision is often a source of great debate. It usually starts with someone arguing to set

b. This lifeline can, of course, be extended by capital providers if they believe that other objectives (e.g., growth) matter more than profitability or that costs will come down over time with better scale economics or other structural changes. We believe that profitability has generally been undervalued as an indicator of organizational health, particularly in early-stage companies.

price as close to WTP as possible in order to maximize profit and preserve company viability. This perspective is usually followed by more moderate voices that argue to set price somewhere in the middle, between WTP and cost. Eventually, the customer champions jump in with passionate justification for even lower prices (typically above cost, but not by much) in order to attract more customers and make up for low margins with volume.

These debates are often passionate because there's no universally correct answer. The argument for maximizing profits is perhaps obvious, but it can also be good business to leave enough room on the value range to delight loyal, buzz-generating customers. Apple's pricing strategy is a good example of this approach. Apple deliberately prices its products below its customers' sky-high WTP (but still well above cost), generating a form of customer devotion that approaches frenzy.[9] Despite paying a handsome price premium by industry standards, almost everyone leaves an Apple store feeling like a winner. Meanwhile, Apple's profits continue skyward.

Our practical advice is to be like Apple and aim for the middle of the value range, even if you're competing for a segment of the market that's not particularly price sensitive. Great products are built on enduring stakeholder partnerships where companies and customers are increasingly rewarded for the ride they've decided to go on together. Even if it's counterintuitive, leaving value on the table for customers is a way to compensate them for doing their part. It's an expression of trust, love, and belonging, all wrapped into that transactional moment of truth.

This idea is also at the heart of one of our favorite leadership maxims: *create more value than you capture.* Legendary entrepreneur and open source pioneer Tim O'Reilly has been challenging tech companies with this phrase for the last few decades.[10] We think this advice is a clarifying principle for anyone building any organization, and certainly anyone seeking to lead one.

All this is to say that price is not simply a technical decision you make with your strategy team, informed by what you can get away with. It's also a proxy for your commitment to be in service to your customers. You're in this together, and the price of doing business with you should reflect that truth.

Looking at leadership through a value lens, the responsibility of a leader is to create value for *others*. You will of course want to capture some of that value for yourself, but the capturing part is not about leadership. Capturing is about survival and security and wealth creation. We make no attributions about those pursuits—indeed, they are necessary—but we want to be clear about the distinction. You create value as a leader, and then capture some of it as an individual. And so our modification to O'Reilly's challenge might be to get out there and create *a whole lot* more value than you capture.

Enter your suppliers

At the other end of the value spectrum are your suppliers. Suppliers are the people and organizations providing things like labor and raw materials and office space, the sugar and eggs to the value cake you've now so thoughtfully sliced up and shared with your customers. The size of that cake of course depends heavily on how much you pay your suppliers for their inputs. The less you pay, the more cake you've got, and vice versa.

So how much should you be shelling out? Just as pricing works best with an understanding of customer WTP, costing works best with an understanding of supplier willingness to sell (WTS). WTS is the *lowest* amount a supplier is willing to accept for their goods and services. If the amount you offer is lower than your suppliers' WTS, even a penny under, they'll walk. Everything between this minimum WTS threshold and what you ultimately pay (your

FIGURE 5-4

Strategic value stick

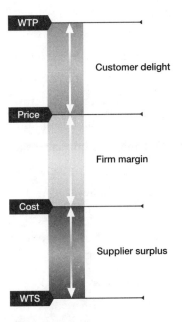

Source: Adam M. Brandenburger and Harborne W. Stuart, "Value-based Business Strategy," *Journal of Economics & Management Strategy* 5 (March 1996): 5–24.

cost) represents supplier surplus. In figure 5-4, we add these additional variables to the mix. In its full glory, this framework is called a *value stick*.

To review, the lower you can get your costs, the more value there is to distribute between you and your customers. So should you squeeze your suppliers to reduce cost as much as possible without crossing their WTS threshold? Large retailers and major players in the auto industry are notorious for this approach, and you will find lots of reasonable people telling you it's your birthright for gaining market power.

We don't advise squeezing until it hurts for the simple reason that it's a lot harder to sustain your company's health without happy, prosperous suppliers. They generally aren't going to stick around or work hard for you if they're not rewarded for it, and so protecting supplier surplus can be just as strategic as leaving value on the table for your customers.

We have observed that too many businesses underestimate the return on delighting their suppliers. One company that doesn't make this mistake is Zappos, the service-crazed online retailer that flamboyantly defies industry norms when it comes to suppliers. Zappos CEO Tony Hsieh is super clear about the rationale for investing in healthy supplier relationships: when your suppliers can't thrive and make a profit, they start making choices that are bad for you, like cutting back on service and innovation. And when suppliers *can* thrive—as in Zappos's case—Hsieh estimates the number of benefits as roughly "endless."[11]

The company walks the talk in its supplier relationships. Zappos returns vendor calls within a few hours. Vendors who visit the company's Las Vegas headquarters are picked up from the airport by a Zappos employee and treated like royalty when they arrive on site. They're thrown a blowout vendor appreciation party every year at a club on the famed Vegas strip. Zappos even gives vendors access to the company's own performance data, which helps them run their own companies better while becoming better suppliers to Zappos. And when it comes to negotiating price, Hsieh honors supplier surplus as the strategic input that it is: "Instead of pounding the vendors, we collaborate. We decide together . . . the amount of risk we want to sign up for, and how quickly we want the business to grow."[12]

This same logic applies to all of your suppliers, including your labor suppliers. For most companies, this means your employees, a reminder that HR decisions can be as strategic as anything else we've discussed.[c] Which brings us to an essential question: What *should* you pay for a steady supply of good labor?

---

c. By the way, complicating reality further, your *customers* can also be a source of labor. The last time you tested your relationship with a loved one by trying to assemble that IKEA shelf together, you were performing a final manufacturing step that trained professionals do in most companies.

As a floor, you *must* pay your employees a living wage, full stop. But there's also a powerful case for going above and beyond that minimum threshold. In her breakthrough "good jobs" research, MIT professor Zeynep Ton demonstrates the performance return on investing in decent wages and dignified jobs, even in low-cost, low-margin business models.[13]

She blows up the assumption that companies that compete on price don't have the luxury of taking care of their employees. A classic Ton example is QuikTrip, an Oklahoma-based chain of convenience stores. Now an $11 billion company with more than eight hundred stores in eleven states, QuikTrip pays low-skilled employees mid-market wages, cross-trains them to perform different types of work, and empowers them to make decisions that matter in the absence of hands-on supervision.[14] These investments lead to higher engagement, higher productivity, and higher retention, which then leads to lower operating costs elsewhere in the business. Ton also makes the connection from these investments to higher sales and more satisfied customers. The end result is that companies like QuikTrip are prospering *because of* higher labor costs, not in spite of them.

Rather than treat their employees like unreliable, interchangeable cost units, the companies Ton studies are investing unapologetically in their frontline people. They're reducing operating costs *and* growing their employee surplus in the form of high wages, while fostering cultures of community and belonging in the workplace. By the way, one benefit of a great culture is that it actually pushes *down* employee WTS, which then grows their value surplus even more.[d] According to Ton, these choices generate an abundance of

---

d. This is somewhat counterintuitive, so we'll give you a simple example: Frances took a pay cut to join the Harvard Business School faculty from another institution, which she was more than happy to do because of the nonfinancial rewards of being at HBS, including great colleagues, great students, dynamism of the classroom, and so on. Her wages went down, but her delight increased threefold (conservatively).

workforce delight that attracts and retains the best people in a talent market and unleashes them to make the business better.[15] As she said to us one morning, during a walk along the Charles River (the only way we could catch her, as the entire world is excited about her work), "These aren't just good jobs, they're *great* jobs. And the firms that provide them are winning *because* of them."

Ton's research is a provocative counterpoint to assumptions embedded in many of today's business models, including the so-called "gig economy." The standard gig business model creates a massive amount of customer delight by meeting a basic human need (e.g., food, transportation, the trash bags you just ran out of) with lightning fast, push-button convenience, all for ludicrously low prices. Because many of these services appear undifferentiated to the market, low price has emerged as a key competitive attribute, delighting consumers even further.

The model seems to work as long as labor suppliers—contractors providing the final, consumer-facing step in the service—can capture a reasonable surplus.[16] Many companies have struggled to pull this off, but an inspirational exception is TaskRabbit, the company that in many ways *launched* the gig economy. One of the lessons of TaskRabbit's evolution is that even gig companies can create business models where everyone wins: customers, companies, and, yes, even suppliers.

Strategic transformation at TaskRabbit

TaskRabbit CEO Stacy Brown-Philpot (remember her from chapter 1?) made the leap from Google to TaskRabbit (initially in the COO role) when she felt a calling to do something new. She was captivated by the chance to empower an organization: "How can I help a community of people do something more than they could otherwise accomplish on their own?"[17] The breakthrough business model she encountered at TaskRabbit had proven you could build a business that connected consumers to freelance workers, but there were cracks in the model that Brown-Philpot felt she could address. Almost a decade of slaying growth-related dragons at Google had prepared her for the role.

TaskRabbit was founded in 2008 to create a space where supply and demand could be met for everyday tasks. The company connected people who could do stuff—known as "taskers"—to people who needed to get stuff done. Tasks ranged from housecleaning to running errands to assembling IKEA furniture, one of the company's most frequent requests. Customers could outsource the jobs they didn't have time or expertise to complete, and flexibility-loving taskers could generate income on a when-they-wanted-to-work basis.

Matching taskers with jobs originally happened through an auction-like system. Clients would post jobs, and taskers would bid against each other to perform them. The model reliably generated a list of competitively priced bids for users, who then chose their tasker based largely on price and availability. In the language of strategy, the auction system had the effect of generating value for customers at the top of the value stick by shrinking the surplus of its supplier-taskers. Although magic was happening at the high end of the tasker skill spectrum, where taskers were often well compensated for their expertise, many lower-skilled taskers were being bid down in a race-to-the-bottom to offer the cheapest possible price for their labor. (See figure 5-5.)

It also took a long time for taskers to sort through jobs and find the ones they wanted—taskers spent, on average, two hours a week searching open tasks. The time and pain of dealing with the system were additional burdens, and so while user and tasker numbers were at their highest in 2013, there was some troubling news buried underneath this headline: the company's fulfillment rate was only

FIGURE 5-5

The original TaskRabbit value stick

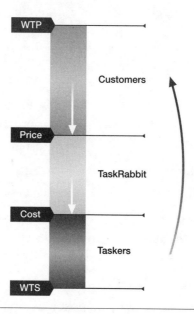

50 percent. In other words, one out of two customer tasks were not finding taskers willing to do them.[18]

To address this problem, Brown-Philpot started at the bottom of the value stick, exploring ways to expand and protect supplier surplus. In a new platform model the company created, taskers were empowered to set their own hourly rates, which could no longer be lower than the markets' minimum wage. Taskers also set their own schedules and made clear the kind of jobs they wanted to do. In this new model, instead of spending hours on the site trying to match their skills and interests with market demand, the company now did the bulk of that work for them.

The result was a more reliable surplus for taskers, but this also meant higher average prices for users. To make these prices palatable for the market, Brown-Philpot knew that increased fulfillment rates would go a long way. But in order to preserve—or even increase—the amount of delight customers experienced, the company also streamlined the user experience to make the customer's hiring process faster and easier to use. The changes helped to increase customer WTP by enabling users to find a qualified tasker in a single visit to the site. (See figure 5-6.)

The new model was a wild success in London, the first place it was tested, a greenfield market where the company could avoid the pain of retraining stakeholders on a new system. User numbers in London grew three times faster than in other markets, and clients doubled the amount they spent on tasks.[19] The number of repeat

FIGURE 5-6

Improved TaskRabbit value stick

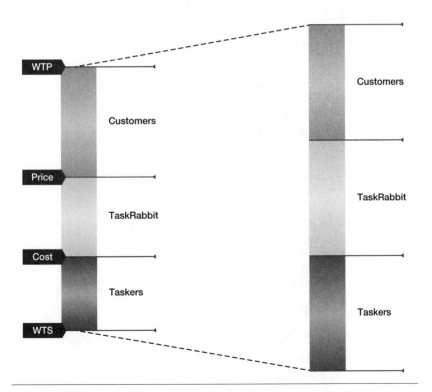

customers was also significantly higher, along with overall client satisfaction and user sentiment. And the all-important fulfillment rate grew to 90 percent.[20]

As the company rolled out the model to existing sites, Brown-Philpot overcame an initial backlash from taskers who worried about losing income. The experience taught her hard-earned lessons about managing change, including the importance of communication, particularly when suppliers' livelihoods are on the line. It also reinforced the value of staying close to what suppliers are thinking and feeling. She created a Tasker advisory council and invites employees to both hire Taskers for their own needs and perform tasks themselves. If you order the service today, there's a chance Brown-Philpot herself may show up.

Once she scaled the new model to all TaskRabbit markets, Brown-Philpot noticed something else surprising: instead of simply competing with each other, taskers were starting to *help* each other, holding classes and posting videos about how to earn more income through more specialized tasks. This created more opportunities for taskers to learn and grow (at virtually no cost to the company). Taskers were finding new meaning in their jobs by unleashing potential in each other, a leadership flywheel that was empowering people—*lots* of people—in Brown-Philpot's absence.

Defy strategic gravity

This is where value-based strategy gets even more interesting. The goal of strategy is to grow the "wedges" on your product's value stick (customer delight, firm margin, and supplier surplus) *without making any of the other wedges smaller*. We call them wedges because it helps people visualize the opportunity for expansion and contraction. It's relatively easy to grow one wedge by shrinking another one. That's what cable companies do when they raise consumer prices—and fury—without doing anything to increase our WTP.[21] Great strategy asks you to work harder than that and find ways to grow everyone's wedge.

One classic way to achieve this is by driving up your customers' WTP, a challenge that has consumed strategists since markets were invented. Whenever you make your products better, cooler, easier to use, more fun, more convenient, and so on, you're putting upward pressure on your customers' WTP for them. This gives you the option to raise prices and enjoy higher margins, while also increasing how much delight your customers experience.

Additional strategies for increasing WTP include better branding and storytelling. They include finding or designing great complements (the ketchup to your hotdogs) and leveraging network effects (more users, more value). They include ideas that could fill entire books, collectively entire WTP libraries, and our objective here is not to add to this impressive catalogue. Instead, we want to remind you that strategy is an extension of who you are as a leader. As impersonal as the language of strategy sometimes sounds, with its forces and sticks and wedges, strategy embeds your humanity into the behavior of your company. It allows you to empower anyone, wherever they may be in your organization, including places you could never reach on your own.

That's what Toyota did when it decided to cooperate with its suppliers rather than compete with them. Toyota broke from the auto industry's norm of brutalizing OEM suppliers and committed to making them better off instead.[22] The calculation was simple, clear-eyed, industrial math: more efficient suppliers would mean lower costs for Toyota. And so Toyota gave its suppliers access to the wisdom of its famed Toyota Production System (TPS). Suppliers got to learn from TPS how to lower their own operating costs, while Toyota got a progressively lower price on parts. This extraordinary learning partnership gave suppliers the chance to expand their surplus not only with Toyota, but also with every other client they served.

Again, we challenge you to bring this type of thinking to your relationships with all of your stakeholders. As you explore ways to stretch the middle of your value stick by lowering *internal* costs, we invite you to think particularly hard about employee compensation. This doesn't necessarily mean bigger paychecks, although that investment may very well be in your strategic best interest (again, see Ton's research for inspiration). Keep in mind that you may also be able to expand employee delight by giving people more flexibility, more autonomy, more opportunities to upskill and learn. You may be able to find ways to put mission and meaning at the center of the employee experience, which have been proven in countless studies to be as important to many people as the salary they're paid.[23]

We offer you these anecdotal, illustrative examples—more like parables—to challenge the widespread assumption that in order for you to win as a company, someone else has to lose. We believe that you can align the interests of customers, shareholders, employees, and suppliers, particularly if you take a holistic, long-term view of your organization. In the next section, we give you the chance to test that idea end explore empowering strategies for your own organization. As you begin, get very clear on the fact that most people will be making most of their decisions without you. How will you design a strategy that will lead them in your absence? How will that strategy reflect who you are as a leader?

Find your wedge

In our experience, great strategy is creative, innovative, and above all, optimistic. Leaders who get it right refuse to accept that the gains of their customers or employees have to come at their company's expense. They refuse to treat their suppliers as competitors scrapping it out for a fixed pie of resources. Instead, as world-class strategists, they strive to stretch the value stick and make everyone better off.

We've found that a simple exercise can help you spark this kind of strategic thinking in yourself and your organization. The exercise works well in both small and large groups (we've done it with hundreds of people at once), and it's one answer to the perennial question of what to do at your next strategic planning offsite. For anyone who dreads that annual ritual, this one's for you.

Sit down with your colleagues in groups of two to four people and do the following:

1. *Tell your company's wedge story.* Look back at the history of your organization and use the value stick framework to describe the major plot points in your strategic story. Which "wedge" formed the basis for your original strategy? How did that strategy evolve over time and which stakeholders gained and lost value along the way? Which wedge do you prioritize now? At whose expense?

2. *Come up with a* new *idea that expands at least one wedge without shrinking any of the others.* The idea here is to create space for new ideas, so try to push yourselves to greenfield thinking. Dwell in the possibility of future wedges. Some questions to prompt your creativity: How could you delight your customers without increasing costs by much (if at all)? How might you help your suppliers use less time or capital in their delivery of great service to you? Could paying your employees more help you lower costs elsewhere in the business? Are there ways to make your employees' happier *without* paying them more?

3. *Present your best idea and invite pushback.* Once you have brought your best ideas and arguments to a place you like, present them to the rest of the team. Use the value stick framework to describe the trade-offs and payoffs. Which wedges are impacted? Which remain untouched? Use the feedback you receive to sharpen your thinking and make your ideas even stronger.

4. *Pilot at least one idea coming out of this exercise.* Send a strong "How about now?" signal and reward creative thinking by executing quickly on the best one or two ideas to come out of the exercise. Frame it as a pilot and put mechanisms in place to learn quickly from the outcomes.

Use your words

True confession: we love the show *Shark Tank*. We love that the outsized energy and possibility of entrepreneurship—something that has brought so much color and shape to our own lives—is the animating force of the show. We love that the show's "sharks," investors who are pitched by contestants on early-stage companies, engage just as vigorously with the African American couple making products for curly hair as the white guy trying to build a better beer cozy. It's a stylized, made-for-TV version of the world we want to live in, one where good ideas compete on their own merits for capital and attention, regardless of the identity of their originators. (Some advice to future *Shark Tank* participants: make sure you're properly valuing the potential upside of having a shark on your team. A shark's dollar is worth more than other dollars.)

We also love that there can be moments of pedagogical magic in an episode. Almost every concept we've explored in this chapter has a good *Shark Tank* analog. When Aaron Krause invented Scrub Daddy, a clever sponge that's soft in warm water and hard and scrubby in cold, he found a way to spike our WTP over traditional sponges without adding much cost. When guest shark Alli Webb, founder of Drybar, reluctantly said no to an investment in Curl-Mix, we saw the emotions that often accompany alignment tensions. Webb appeared to love the entrepreneurs and their business model, but she was in the business of straightening hair, not making curly hair look great, which was CurlMix's value proposition.

One part of strategy that repeatedly gets a spotlight on the show is the importance of being able to communicate strategy quickly and persuasively, in language that everyone can understand. Your plan has to be as accessible to a shark who may know little about your industry as it is to the viewers keeping up at home. If you can't describe simply how you're going to win as a business, there's almost no point in showing up and getting into the tank.

We believe the same is true in the real world of leadership. To put this in starker terms, nothing we've discussed in this chapter matters if the rest of the people in the organization don't understand your strategy well enough to make their own decisions based on it. As we said in the beginning, strategy guides discretionary behavior *to the limit of how well you communicate it*. So, let's talk about how to communicate it.

The goal here is to understand deeply so that you can describe simply. If you understand your strategy deeply but can only describe it in a complex or jargony way, then you only get to talk to the subset of your organization that speaks that esoteric language. If you understand your strategy only superficially, then it will not survive out in the wild, in dynamic conditions where the pressure to abandon the plan is relentless. Your people will be continuously tempted to deviate from the strategy—usually for excellent reasons, like responding to a customer service request. A strategic North Star, simply described, gives us all a fighting chance at staying the course.

Pick any mode(s) of communication you want and certainly play to your strengths. Every year Jeff Bezos writes a long letter to his shareholders in which he reinforces the pillars of Amazon's strategy. It's addressed to investors who own a piece of the company but clearly written for every stakeholder in his orbit. Bezos is a clear, persuasive writer, and these annual letters are a great example of "deeply/simply" communication.

In his 2017 shareholder letter, Bezos reminded everyone of his internal ban on slide presentations in favor of long-form, six-page, double-sided memos that Amazon executives draft to pitch new ideas to each other. Memos are drafted collaboratively and circulated without the authors' names, to minimize politics. Strategy meetings at Amazon start with everyone reading every word of a "six-pager" and then engaging with the ideas in what one Amazon alumnus recalled as "the most efficient and exciting meetings I had ever attended for any company."[24] When was the last time you described a meeting that way? Efficient? Exciting?

Bezos has called this practice as the smartest thing he ever did, since the discipline of crafting sentences and paragraphs forces deeper thinking.[25] We tend to think of writing as a tool for influencing others, but writing is also the greatest tool for sorting out our own thoughts that human beings have invented.[26] If you want to create a better strategy, we advise writing about it early and often. Start with a blank page and give yourself real time and space (think days, not hours) to develop your ideas. Share what you've written with your colleagues so they can help you improve your logic—and so you can start influencing their choices, even in your absence. (See the sidebar "An Ode to Old-School Strategy Communication Tools, aka 'Books.'")

An Ode to Old-School Strategy Communication Tools, aka "Books"

One of the best strategic communicators we've encountered in our work is Jan Carlzon, the CEO who turned around Scandinavian Airlines (SAS) in the 1980s. In a gift to strategists everywhere, Carlzon documented the turnaround in fantastic detail in his book *Moments of Truth*.[27] We teach excerpts of this book in the HBS classroom so that students can see what it means, on a day-to-day basis, to change behavior at the scale of a sprawling, twenty-thousand-person organization.

Carlzon has thought deeply about the role of strategic communications, particularly when it comes to empowerment leadership: "A leader communicating a strategy to thousands of decentralized decision-makers who must then apply that general strategy to specific situations must go much further. Rather than merely issuing your message, you have to be certain that every employee has truly absorbed it."[28] One way Carlzon achieved this at SAS was through a red-covered booklet he wrote titled *Let's Get in There and Fight*, which the company eventually started calling "the little red book." It was a small, illustrated, comic-style book that used few words, big type, and a cartoon airplane to explain the company's shift to a market-oriented strategy anchored on delighting business travelers. The little red book's storyline honored the past, articulated a change mandate, and provided an optimistic way forward, a three-part structure we have seen work again and again in turnaround situations.

According to Carlzon, he was surrounded by skeptics who thought that SAS's highly educated, intellectual workforce would reject such a

(continued)

simple communication tool. In fact, the opposite happened. The book was embraced up and down the hierarchy, reinforcing Carlzon's view that "there is no such thing as oversimplified." Three years after the little red book's debut, SAS came out of its nosedive, increasing revenue fivefold with an industry-leading profit margin and rapidly improving customer satisfaction, particularly among business travelers.

We've worked with executive teams all over the world on drafting their own versions of the little red book, and we've seen immediate impact in industries that range from retail to health care to energy. (One multinational firm we worked with finally broke a strategic logjam that had been in place for years after senior leaders worked through this exercise.) As you try writing your own, we suggest limiting your first draft to just three pages: The Good Ol' Days, The Change Mandate, and The Optimistic Way Forward. Choose language and pictures that a loved one at home would understand, someone with only passing exposure to the industry. Write multiple drafts and only then layer in more pages once the story holds together.

If you question the relevance of books and pages in an age of digital communications, we'll refer you to Marguerite Zabar Mariscal, Momofuku's visionary, 30-something CEO. Mariscal commissioned beautifully designed, pocket-size "guidebooks" once the company reached a thousand employees. It was the scale at which she could no longer rely on direct exposure to leadership to teach people what made Momofuku's restaurants special.[29] Mariscal created a powerful new tool for leading in her absence, using the oldest trick in the book (wink).

Of course, words and pictures aren't the only ways in which you can communicate as a leader. Your actions scream louder than anything else, and we invite you to use that bodily megaphone, well, *strategically*. When Herb Kelleher refused to transfer those bags, the news rocketed around every Southwest check-in counter, faster than any memo could have, reminding employees of the bag transfer policy. When Stacy Brown-Philpot quietly joins the ranks of her taskers, she's reminding everyone in the company that TaskRabbit's front line is essential to the success of the business.

Hiroshi Mikitani, CEO of Rakuten, transformed the Tokyo-based, e-commerce giant by embracing English as the company's common tongue. Convinced that adopting the "business language of the world" was critical to globalizing the company, Mikitani used the full force of his CEO position to change workforce behavior at extraordinary scale, a campaign called "Englishnization" that our colleague Tsedal Neeley documented in her riveting book.[30] Mikitani rolled out a system of incentives and disincentives (including demotion for linguistic resisters) that got everyone speaking English in record time. But the most impactful choice he made may have been to stop speaking Japanese himself at the office, even in one-on-one conversations with Japanese colleagues with whom he had worked for decades. Mikitani was betting the company's future on English, and his message could not have been clearer. According to Neeley, "he was committed enough—and courageous enough—to model the change he envisioned in every single interaction."

The emperor's got clothes

The most effective strategic leaders we've observed are Mikitani-esque, internalizing their strategies so deeply that they inform their most fundamental choices. A former CEO of Vanguard once showed up in Frances's office in a threadbare suit and shoes that had clearly been resoled multiple times. He had traveled there from the company's headquarters through some ungodly mix of indirect flights, airport shuttles, and subway rides. Vanguard's strategy is to be the lowest-cost player in the financial services space, which it achieves through a unique, customer-owned structure and companywide obsession with efficiency. Frances asked him very directly: "So is this just for show or are you really this frugal?" He essentially answered, "It's both." When you step up to the leadership challenge, whether you like it or not, there's no option to turn off the broadcast feature on your actions. Is it who you are or just for show? The answer is always both.

We loved this exchange because it was a reminder of what a strategic leader looks like—literally, someone so committed that their strategy influences the clothes they put on in the morning. It's also an example of using any means necessary to empower the organization to act in its strategic interest. If it takes scuffed-up shoes or speaking a new language or cartoon airplanes to get everyone to work differently, so be it. The best strategists aren't above it.

They're also not above changing the plan. Most strategies have an expiration date, as conditions evolve and your good intentions get roughed up by reality. The minute your competitors improve their products, that attribute map is out of date. As soon as your suppliers innovate or your customers switch up their buying criteria, the borders on your value stick become fluid again. Many companies have an annual strategic planning rite, but 365 days is a very long time to wait to adapt to changes in the behavior of your most critical stakeholders.

If you seek to lead in your absence, then get your strategy right, tell everyone about it, and revisit it early and often. And if you're swinging for maximum absentee impact, pull that other, all-powerful organizational lever: culture. Get your culture working for you rather than against you. That's the focus of our next chapter.

Questions for Reflection

✓ How do your colleagues and/or direct reports—the people you seek to lead—know what to do with their discretionary behavior? How reliant are they on being *told* what to do by people who manage them?

✓ Can you describe your organization's strategy in simple, jargon-free language? Can the people around you?

✓ How do employees learn about your organization's strategy? Can you think of new ways to reinforce that learning?

✓ Can you think of ways for your organization to win without customers, suppliers, or employees losing? How might you create more value for both your company and its major stakeholders?

6

CULTURE

In addition to strategy, culture is the other major lever you have for leading organizations, arguably the more vocal one. Whatever strategy has not made clear to your extended team, culture will unapologetically fill the void. Culture establishes the rules of engagement after leadership leaves the room; it explains how things are *really* done around here.

Culture tells us how to behave in a meeting. It tells us who gets to take up space automatically and who has to work for it. It tells us whether we should follow the rules or cut corners, whether we should share or hoard information, whether we should stick our necks out and try to make things better or simply adapt to the status quo. What's more important, growth or excellence? Action or analysis? Being direct or saving face? Strategy drops hints, but it's culture that has the definitive answers.

Culture carries its guidance to the farthest corners of the organization to places you may never go and people you may never meet. There's a story about the salvation of FedEx that Michael Basch, one of the company's founding officers, likes to tell.[1] In 1973, FedEx was on the ropes, bankruptcy looming, nothing going right fast enough.

The company's iconic founder and CEO, Fred Smith, had done everything he could think of to save the organization, including gambling the only capital he had left in a desperate trip to Las Vegas (astonishingly, this bought him some time). Smith was out of next moves.

As this existential crisis unfolded, a customer called FedEx in tears because her wedding dress hadn't arrived yet, with less than twenty-four hours until the ceremony. A frontline service employee named Diane jumped into action, tracked down the dress, and chartered a small Cessna to deliver it—all without wasting precious time by asking anyone for permission. (We've tried and failed to find her full name.) The gesture created so much buzz at the wedding that it got the attention of some executive guests. The following week, those same guests decided to take a bet on using a young, wobbly FedEx for shipping some of their products, driving up demand from three packages a day to thirty. It was enough to save the company.

FedEx's strategy in these early years was simple: deliver time-sensitive packages with speed and certainty. But Smith and his team had also built a strong, "bleeding purple" (the company's primary logo color) culture marked by a get-it-done ethos and disregard for external signifiers, including race, gender, and company status. Everyone mattered. Everyone had the agency and obligation to contribute in meaningful ways. Diane's bold decision making created a lifeline for FedEx, and it wasn't a charismatic CEO or a well-defined strategy that made the difference. Those things may have pointed out the finish line—deliver packages quickly—but it was culture that unleashed her to go all out.

What *is* culture?

Culture usually becomes "a thing" when people realize that something about their culture needs to change. This awareness often comes later in an organization's life cycle than it should, and part of our mission here is to shorten that timeline. For pedagogical reasons, we're going to simply assume that there's something about the culture of your own organization that you already know you want to change.

Let's start there: If you could change anything about your culture, what would it be? Is there more than one thing on the list? Take a few minutes to think about it and then write down your answers. We ask these questions right up front because the reflection itself can be empowering. Most people—even the most senior leaders—can feel, at times, as if culture is something they have to endure, not something that's within their power to change. They couldn't be more wrong.

As a starting place for discovering how possible it is to change culture, we like former MIT professor Edgar H. Schein's iconic framework, which loosely divides organizational culture into artifacts, behaviors, and shared basic assumptions.[2] As Schein argues persuasively, to get people to reliably *behave* the way you want— even in your absence—you have to get them to reliably *think* the way you want.

David Neeleman famously flew as a crew member once a month when he started JetBlue.[3] He would put on an apron, serve coffee, and introduce himself up and down the aisle with a friendly, "Hi, I'm Dave." Neeleman electrified the organization every time he did this and reinforced the company's shared basic assumptions, including the belief that everyone, at every level, was in service to JetBlue passengers. The most important assumption he surfaced—a somewhat radical idea at the time—was that customers are *people*. JetBlue's mission was to "bring humanity back to air travel." Seeing the CEO treat a passenger like a human being was a warning shot to everyone that no one flies steerage on this airline. *That's how things are really done around JetBlue.*

Another way to describe culture is that it's our collective agreement about what is true. What is important. What is a crisis. What is cause for celebration or pride or shame. Culture even determines something as fundamental as what is funny. Humor is not a universal truth; it's a *cultural* one. For example, a culture challenge at Riot Games was that behaviors that were coded as funny and harmless at an early stage in the company's history, when it was a relatively homogenous group of young, primarily male gamers—things like physical gags—were no longer funny or harmless once more and varied people joined the team. (See the sidebar "Ten Signs You Shouldn't Make That Next Joke.")

Schein once went so far as to say, "The only thing of real importance that leaders do is to create and manage culture."[4] We have a hard time disagreeing with this statement, except maybe quibbling with the "only" part (see chapters 1–5). We'd argue that culture is in the running for most important because—among other things—it stays behind long after you've left the building. You may move on from the company, but a strong culture can endure for generations.

Culture also has incredible reach, spilling out beyond the boundaries of your organization. Culture changes the people it touches, who, in turn, change the people *they* touch, and so on. Anyone who has felt more optimistic after walking into Starbucks—or felt cooler when they chose that indie coffee shop instead—knows that culture can influence anyone who interacts with it. If your ambition as a leader is maximum impact, then learn to become a culture warrior.

Among the most effective culture warriors walking the planet is Patty McCord, former chief talent officer at Netflix. You won't find empty values statements on the walls of a Netflix conference room, not on McCord's watch. As she helped to build Netflix into a media giant, McCord articulated the behaviors the company prized most—there are nine—and then used them to drive all hiring, compensation, and exit decisions. She socialized new recruits on these behaviors in a famous hundred-slide presentation on Netflix's unique culture, and then reinforced them constantly, for example, invoking "honesty" (number eight) if colleagues withheld feedback from each other. (Sheryl Sandberg described McCord's presentation, known as the Netflix Culture Deck, as "the most important document ever to come out of [Silicon] Valley."[5]) McCord also challenged employees to question each other's actions if they were inconsistent with Netflix culture, an act she explicitly labeled an expression of "courage" (number six). By the time McCord left the company after more than a decade in her role, Netflix was behaving exactly as she and CEO Reed Hastings had designed it to behave: curious (number four), innovative (number five), and passionate (number seven). Not long after McCord made her culture deck public, Netflix dropped a complete season of *House of Cards* and forever changed the way the world consumed content.[6]

McCord designed Netflix's culture to attract high-performing creative leaders who thrive in work environments where they have a high degree of freedom and, in McCord's worldview, are so self-motivated, self-aware, and self-disciplined that they're also worthy of that freedom. These "innovator-mavericks" (her preferred term) hate almost everything about being trapped in a typical role or organization. They don't want to be told what to do with their discretionary behavior, and they're certainly not wasting time reading the company handbook. They even resist restrictions such as vacation or expense policies, which Netflix has essentially abolished. The company's expense policy is, "Act in Netflix's best interest."

McCord did everything in her power to lure these autonomous creatures into the building and then set them free with a culture that told them everything they needed to know. She and Hastings stayed out of their way and made sure everyone else did, too. In other words, the most senior executives at Netflix were often *intentionally* absent, leading from the sidelines, where their most valuable, freedom-loving employees preferred them to be. It's a model that

Ten Signs You Shouldn't Make That Next Joke

We're going to be super-directive in this section, since humor remains a source of cultural confusion inside many organizations. To be clear, we believe that laughter is essential to surviving the absurdity of being human, to say nothing of going to work every day. However, to use humor in a leadership role is a varsity sport, and our standard counsel is that you should only come off the bench if you have reason to believe you're pretty good at it. The following ten signs suggest that you may not be ready for the big leagues:

1. **You've recently used the phrase "just kidding."** When workplace humor works, there's no ambiguity about your good intentions. If you find yourself saying, "I'm kidding!" (or some similar variation) on a regular basis, then the chance you're crossing lines is high. In most cases, what you really should be saying is, "I'm sorry."

2. **You scan your audience before proceeding.** If you have to look around and make sure you're "OK" before being funny, then it's probably not worth the risk or reward at work. Save it for a hometown crowd that's going to give you the benefit of the doubt, like a good friend or loved one, although you may be overconfident with those segments, too.

3. **The nonverbal signals from your audience are mixed.** People aren't shy in revealing whether humor is working for them, but you have to pay attention. Is their body language open or closed? Are they meeting your gaze or looking away? If you don't have confident answers to these questions, then give yourself a humor time-out.

4. **The punchline has something to do with someone else's body.** The most obvious transgressions in this category are being corrected by public norms (see growing body positivity movement), but there's still work to be done here. Our simple rule is to keep all observations about someone else's body to yourself. And you don't get a free pass if you're a straight man talking about another straight man's height, weight, hair, relationship with the gym, or the way an article of clothing fits him.

5. **You laugh first or loudest to make sure everyone gets it.** Humor should be able to stand on its own and do the work for you. That's the point. It's not a great sign if you have to regularly lead the witness in order to get people to laugh.

6. **You rely heavily on the punchline "Too soon?"** Full disclosure, we've been guilty of this one in the past. While an unexpected, well-placed "Too soon?" can be comedy gold, if it becomes a go-to phrase, then you may be getting too comfortable with other people's discomfort.

7. **It involves a gag, prank, or practical joke.** We're going to keep this one simple and say just don't do it at work. We'll make an exception if you're a brilliant comedian, have your own daytime talk show, and have been making a wide variety of viewers laugh for over a decade. (See any episode of *The Ellen Show*.) Everyone else should resist the temptation to jump out at their colleagues from behind a plant.

8. **Your joke would have killed at an earlier stage in the company's life cycle.** What everyone agreed was funny when you

(continued)

were a smaller, more homogenous organization may no longer be OK. Like other elements of organizational culture, humor often needs to evolve as the company matures and diversifies.

9. **Your record as a bystander is mixed.** If you tend to laugh along with a group, even when you know a comment is unacceptable, then your instincts are not particularly reliable. A note to all bystanders: don't leave the impression that you're complicit. If it's too uncomfortable to make a stand, then make an exit. Doing nothing plays as an endorsement.

10. **Your jokes tend to come at the expense of other people.** This sounds obvious, but when workplace humor is used effectively, it sparks joy, connection, and insight, *and it does no harm.* A comedic human sacrifice can be tempting, but it can hurt both individuals and cultures. Among other things, you're signaling that a person's boundaries and well-being can be casually violated.

reveals another foundational truth about leadership: some of your best people don't always *want* you in the room. Culture gives you the confidence to exit.

Do you have a culture problem?

By June of 2017, the mandate to change the culture at Uber could not have been stronger. This was not lost on then-CEO Travis Kalanick. As reported by Mike Isaac in *Super Pumped: The Battle for Uber,* while Kalanick was on leave, he drafted an email to the company that he never ended up sending.[a] The email was humbled and reflective, mirroring the version of Kalanick we had gotten to know earlier that spring. He opened with a sober take on Uber's culture challenges: "Over the last seven years, our company has grown a lot—but it hasn't grown up."[7]

Kalanick took responsibility for the company's cultural missteps, including its emphasis on growth at all costs and its transactional approach to stakeholder relationships. He acknowledged that the values that had driven Uber to its surreal, historic positioning— to becoming the most valuable startup in the world—also had an unanticipated downside. "There's a lot of good intent behind our values," he wrote, but he conceded that they had also been misused and misinterpreted. And then he used a descriptor for this distortion that would have gotten everyone's attention: "weaponized."

This word is sometimes used too casually, but it wasn't in Uber's case. Here's our definition of a weaponized value: it's the manipulation of an espoused value to disempower, or in extreme cases, harm someone. It's the opposite of leadership in that it's all about the weaponizer and their own interests. A weaponized value dresses up a new belief in the guise of an old one. It changes the meaning of *what is true* without the rest of the organization's consent. For example, we worked with one company that listed "default to trust" among its core values. This phrase was meant to remind everyone to give each other the benefit of the doubt, a noble idea, but it began to be used to shut down healthy dissent. "Default to trust," a manager might say to a direct report who questioned the plan or offered an alternative viewpoint.

It was clear that there were parts of Uber's culture that had indeed been weaponized, which was one of the reasons Kalanick

a. By this point Uber's board of directors had begun the process of removing Kalanick as CEO.

invited Frances to join the team. We still fantasize about what might have been if we had gotten the call earlier, whether we could have helped to head off some of the pain the company went through. In our experience, a pattern of weaponization is a lagging indicator of an unhealthy culture. Our goal is to give you the tools to diagnose and change culture before this critical phase, at the point when your culture simply needs to be repaired (rather than stripped to the studs for a gut renovation).

How do you know when you're at a cultural moment of truth? The trite answer is that people will often tell you. When Susan Fowler endured her very, very strange year at Uber, she reported her experiences internally well before she chose to share them publicly.[8] The facts of her case never made it all the way to Kalanick, from what we understand, but because of the courage of Fowler and other culture whistleblowers, we now live in a world where feedback on culture is finally making its way to all the people who need to hear it.

It helps that culture has become a relatively well-understood concept, thanks in part to workplace norms that have placed it at the center of the talent wars. Great employees want to work in environments where their values are aligned with their employer's, and they're increasingly vocal about demanding it. If you suspect your culture needs a refresh, we advise being super-direct with your colleagues. Ask them what about your existing culture is and is not working. Chase down the answer with the conviction that Schein might be right and it's the most important thing you do as a leader.

The goal in these discussions is to develop a reasonable hypothesis that you can then test more systematically (see the "Culture Change Playbook" section later in the chapter). We suggest gathering this informal data in intimate, interactive formats such as small groups or one-on-one discussions. Start with the empathy anchors on your team, the people who are naturally wired into the experiences of others. Include the truth tellers and people with nothing to lose. Add a culture discussion to all exit interviews. (A question we've found particularly useful in exit interviews is, "As someone who cares deeply about the culture here, is there anything you think I should know about your experience or the experiences of other people?") Control for status, function, and anything else that might be a variable in how people experience *what is true*. If you have reason to believe you won't get an honest answer—if psychological safety isn't a cultural given—then do what it takes to protect the messengers.

As you develop your intuition, here are some conversational entry points that we've seen work:

- How well do you think our culture sets people up for success? Are there ways that it also undermines their effectiveness?

- Have any of our values or commitments to each other become "empty" or even "weaponized"?

- How aligned is our culture with our current challenges and opportunities?

- What do we need to change culturally to achieve our most ambitious goals?

A more difficult part of this intuition-building process can be to listen—*really* listen—to what you hear in these discussions, with the curiosity of an anthropologist and the radical accountability of a leader. Listen as someone responsible for the experiences of others, both in your presence and in your absence. Listen without your ego or internal defenses getting in the way. The objective is to convince yourself you need a culture shift before you prepare to convince others.

The Case for Examining Your Own Sh*t

Here's the thing: the rules of engagement operating inside your organization did not come out of nowhere. More often than not, they came from the experiences of the individuals who shaped your culture, the assumptions driving their own behavior. In other words, the roots of a company's collective agreement about *what is true* can be found in the hearts, minds, and personal histories of its leaders.

The most effective culture leaders we know use their experiences as a jumping-off point, but (and here's the real trick) they don't get trapped by them. They remain open to the idea that what their own life has taught them—the assumptions and behaviors driving their *personal* triumphs and failures—may not be aligned with their company's current culture needs. For example, we often see variations of Kalanick's "always be hustlin'" value built into the cultures of companies with founders still on the payroll. This is understandable, as leading an organization from concept to success is an extraordinary achievement, one that's often powerfully formative for the people involved. Few entrepreneurs pull it off, none of them without hustling. Why shouldn't we all keep "hustlin'"?

Well, there may be a few good reasons: your company may now be at a stage where it needs to operate more systematically, or certain teams (for example, legal) may need the cultural freedom to adopt a different mindset. Instead of hustling all day long, you may want your general counsel thinking rigorously about how to protect company stakeholders. The point is to have the mental flexibility to pivot when your learned assumptions diverge from the behavioral requirements of the organization. It's to unleash *yourself* as a leader by refusing to play exclusively within the boundaries of your own experiences.

This kind of agility requires you to recognize your own beliefs and their impact, which can be some of the hardest work you do as a leader. We approach prescriptions for getting there with humility: one person's delightful weekend of intensive self-improvement is another person's hellscape. (Between the two of us, we embody the poles of this scale.) Regardless of where you fall on this spectrum, there's a good case for bringing other people into your reflective process, people who can help identify patterns that are hard to see in ourselves.[9] For now, before you resume the activities of a culture warrior on a larger scale, pause and focus on yourself as the object of inquiry, even for a few moments. Applying Schein's framework to your own personal "culture," we offer some questions to begin the process. The objective here is not to reach definitive answers, but to start creating space for a more conscious boundary between you and your organization:

- Which behaviors and assumptions have been most important to your success as a leader? If we were to interview you about how you "made it," which of those would show up in the stories you tell?

- Try writing them down as headlines; for example, "Move fast," "Never settle," "Stay hungry." Have some fun with it and imagine the inspirational office art you might design to broadcast the message (Birds in flight! Rowers pulling together as dawn breaks!). Which words and images would you use?

- How aligned are your headlines with your company's current challenges? Do you see any challenges or scenarios where

(continued)

they might be misaligned? Is there anywhere in your organization where you *don't* want to hang your posters?

- As you think about the *future* impact you hope to have as a leader, which of your existing behaviors and assumptions are most important going forward? Do you need to evolve or let go of any of them? Is there anything missing?

In Kalanick's unsent email, he described the mindset he was committed to changing: "I favored logic over empathy . . ." "I approached decisions as transactions . . ." "I was mostly just struggling to survive . . ." In subsequent paragraphs, he continued to take responsibility for how his personal worldview was amplified and projected onto Uber as a company. "I succeeded by acting small," Kalanick wrote, "but failed in being bigger." This kind of tension between what got you *here* and what's going to get you *there*, to the impact you dream of having as a leader, is inside all of us. If Travis Kalanick, the so-called bad boy of tech, can confront it, then so can the rest of us.

Kalanick's infamous "toe-stepping" maxim was one of the first values to be publicly retired when Dara Khosrowshahi took the helm as CEO.[b] As Khosrowshahi explained in a widely read LinkedIn post, "'Toe-stepping' was meant to encourage employees to share their ideas regardless of their seniority or position in

b. Kalanick's original articulation of this value was "meritocracy and toe-stepping," which he explained in a detailed, fifty-page culture document. The language reflected Kalanick's conviction that good ideas could come from anywhere in the company, and lower-ranking employees should have cultural license to "step on the toes" of higher-ranking employees in order to be heard.

the company, but too often it was used as an excuse for being an asshole."[10] He went on to acknowledge an inconvenient truth: that the shared assumptions and behaviors that got Uber *here* were not going to carry the company all the way *there*, to a sustainable, thriving company.

This is incredibly common tension that's not limited to the world of technology startups. Indeed, we believe that some variation on this challenge is at play inside almost every organization. Practically every company we know is relying in some way on assumptions and behaviors that need to be updated to reflect their current reality. Which elements of your culture might be doing more harm than good at this point? Is there anything that got you *here* that's now standing in the way of your ability to go *there*? (See the sidebar "The Case for Examining Your Own Sh*t.")

Soul searching at Riot

In the summer of 2018, the Riot Games leadership team members experienced every modern CEO's nightmare: they woke up to a breaking news story alleging that a broken, sexist culture had emerged on their watch.[11] A few days later, the company issued a public apology and vowed to address the roots of the problem.[12] Riot was known for its loyalty to players of its blockbuster game *League of Legends*, and the company pledged to bring the same level of devotion and empathy to its relationship with employees. It was a sincere, full-throated commitment to change and the reason we agreed to work with the team. Riot's leaders were clear that the assumptions and behaviors that got them *here* needed real reform.

The team's first step was to actively listen. In the days following the article's release, company leadership met with hundreds of "Rioters" in small, interactive sessions to discuss what had gone wrong. A theme that emerged during these emotional conversations was frustration with a high-octane "bro culture" that hadn't evolved along with the company. Riot began as a scrappy, disruptive startup. Its handful of employees identified as underdogs in the gaming industry, channeling passion and ambition into better serving their fellow gamers. The language of an early "Riot Manifesto" focused on animating behaviors like "Challenge Convention." As the company scaled to a workforce of thousands, however, the context surrounding these behaviors was lost. "Challenge Convention" turned into "Challenge Everything." "Take Play Seriously" became license to marginalize colleagues who weren't considered true gamers, a subjective category that too often excluded women.

In addition to listening, Riot leadership commissioned a companywide survey—drafted by a newly formed cultural transformation team—that asked about the culture that would enable Riot to deliver resonant game experiences over the long term. The survey was simple and direct, just three questions:

- Describe the core values you believe would foster the ideal company culture for Riot. Be as specific and descriptive as you like!

- Which elements of Riot's current culture are preventing you from experiencing the culture you just described?

- Which elements of Riot's current culture do you observe are preventing others from experiencing the culture you just described?

Survey responses were raw and real, revealing widespread discomfort with the status quo and a hunger for a more collaborative work environment. Many respondents expressed a desire to scale the company's original vision in more inclusive ways, to adapt its founding values to the diverse workforce Riot needed to achieve its ambitions. One respondent summarized the aspirations of the larger team: "The best version of Riot is a place where Rioters come together with the shared goal of delivering unforgettable experiences for players . . . Our shared passion for games unites us toward a common goal, but our diversity is our strength. Each Rioter has their own wealth of experience and perspective, and an equal seat at the table."[13]

Finally, all employees were invited to optional cultural "visioning" sessions, where they were encouraged to revisit the original Riot Manifesto, an exercise rich with symbolism. The manifesto was the company's most important cultural artifact, and employees were given the mandate to change it, to even blow it up if necessary. Armed with pens and paper, they were asked to design a better culture for themselves and their teammates, one where everyone had an equal opportunity to thrive.

To our surprise, Rioters overwhelmingly wanted to retain the core of the company's original vision. There was broad agreement that many of Riot's founding values were still relevant if truly actualized—if the company truly walked the talk—and if these values were reconciled with what Riot had become, a company now positioned not only to disrupt but also to lead. Today's Riot needed to innovate *and* execute with excellence, to embrace creativity *and* collaborate broadly, to take exquisite care of players *and* each other. These had been trade-offs in the past, but that tension had become untenable.

In December, a few months after the original article was published, Riot leaders shared their new cultural values with the company. Gone was the term "manifesto," with its suggestion of revolutionary zeal, but many other words were familiar. Player experience was still paramount, but language that had been used to undermine trust or justify exclusion had been struck. A new commitment to "thrive together" felt particularly important to people.

The updated values informed the rest of the company's culture change priorities, including the addition of a new chief people officer and chief diversity officer. This new leadership team (two women, one of them a woman of color) proceeded to assess all hiring practices and performance management systems. They invested in an educational foundation for all employees on how to build inclusive, high-performing teams. Their mission was to help create a reality that matched the height of the company's new ideals.

Most exciting to us, Riot's ambition on inclusion has moved beyond its own organizational boundaries. As the company continues to promote belonging inside Riot, Riot leaders have doubled down on fostering inclusion more broadly. The company is leading an initiative to build a working group for diversity and inclusion (D&I) professionals in gaming, and representation in its own games—played by over 80 million people a *month*—is taken as seriously as other creative priorities. As a result, female characters and characters of color have been given more prominence in the company's games. Queer love stories have begun to show up in games' elaborate backstories. A full-time role focused on inclusion in products has been added to Riot's dedicated D&I team, a role unique to the company, as far as we know. Although Riot is proud of its history of representation, these efforts have new resonance. They also reinforce what we love most about culture change: you can't contain it. Culture changes the people it touches, and culture *change* transforms them. The people touched by Riot's extraordinary culture journey are becoming culture warriors themselves.

The Culture Change Playbook

We've done a fair amount of pedagogical "sanding" at this point, hopefully prepping your minds for a fresh, new coat of insight. (Curiously, this remains Frances's favorite education metaphor.)

Let's now take a moment to revisit the question we asked at the beginning of the chapter: If you could change anything about your culture, what would it be?

Before you take the actions we outline next, we suggest repeating the intuition-building steps—the conversations and focus groups we proposed earlier in the chapter—until you're convinced you indeed have a culture problem. Keep in mind that not every organizational problem has a culture solution, but every culture problem has an organizational solution. Said differently, every culture problem can be broken down into its component parts and solved, even the ones that feel the most daunting or sensitive. The process will be no more complex than some of the other initiatives you're leading, so bring your most optimistic, can-do self to the experience.

Once you're ready to proceed, "The Playbook" will help you move from informed conviction to organizational impact, a sequence we've developed and tested over more than a decade of doing this work.

Step 1: Collect the devastating data

Start by describing the problem that culture change will solve. Has safety taken a back seat to other priorities? Are there demographic tendencies in who gets to thrive? Has the company become too cautious? Too transactional? Too complacent? The "devastating" data are simply the observable parts of the problem, the hard evidence that all is not well in the kingdom. Capture it in a format that will allow you to remeasure and demonstrate progress later on.

Step 2: Keep it to yourself (for now)

Resist the temptation to immediately broadcast your findings. This step can be counterintuitive in an age of increasing transparency, but when organizations share tough culture data *without* a productive path forward, they can quickly lose momentum while well-meaning people debate the accuracy and sufficiency of the data (and everyone else gets crazy frustrated). Indeed, we've seen well-meaning organizations lose momentum for *years* when data are shared and debated before there are viable correctives. Share the evidence with enough people to execute step 3, which is to pilot potential solutions. Limit information access to this need-to-know group, just for now.

Step 3: Pilot a rigorous and optimistic way forward

Running a good culture-change pilot program has three core elements: intention, design, and execution.

Your *intention* is to demonstrate that success is possible—to show the organization that the problem can be solved (relatively) quickly without good people being harmed. It's often important to reassure your colleagues at this stage that your objective is not to condemn anyone, but to unleash the organization's full potential. Your starting assumption is that experienced, well-intentioned employees made reasonable choices. If the pilot succeeds, then those same employees will be making choices that are even *more* reasonable. That's the optimistic part.

For the *design* phase, recruit a pilot leadership team with a bias for action and deep intuition about the problem. Decide as a team which organizational behaviors you want to change and the most effective levers for changing them. Channeling Schein again, try to isolate the assumptions that are driving those behaviors. How might you change the way good people think? In our experience, the most enduring change campaigns ultimately impact mindset. That said, it's also fair game at this stage to push directly on behaviors and even on artifacts.

As you move to *execute* the pilot, be as creative and audacious as possible, running smart experiments in a range of conditions. Head off the criticism that you made it too easy on yourselves by choosing a team or location with low barriers to progress. We often advise people to choose the most difficult conditions for the pilot, to drive the steepest learning curve and start winning over the skeptics. Finally, document everything you do and learn. Collect pilot data in a form that supports a persuasive story. How did success show up in the data? How did you know that you built a culture of safety? Of trust? Of inclusion? By the end of the execution phase, you should be able to answer these questions definitively.

Step 4: Involve everyone in the solution

Now you can tell everyone the good news: yes, we have a culture problem, but we also have rigorous, evidence-based insights into the solution. Share the before-and-after pilot data, as well as the detailed story of what you did and learned. Focus the organization on the optimistic way forward, where there are no condemned parties or cynical motives. Invite broad participation in scaling solutions and making them even better. Note that something magical often happens at this stage, with much higher levels of creativity and accelerated action than the pilot team could generate on its own. This is your company unleashed. Embrace it. (See the sidebar "Playbook in Action at Harvard Business School.")

Add "culture" to your title

Culture change is often viewed as important but not urgent, a lofty side hustle you get to pursue only after you've done your day job. But the most successful organizational leaders we know are the ones who put culture at the very center of what they do. They're the CEOs who implicitly replace the "e" with a "c" and interpret their roles as chief

Playbook in Action at Harvard Business School

In less than a year, Frances and her colleagues changed the culture of gender for students at Harvard Business School, a one-hundred-year-old institution where harassment of female students and teachers had become too common.[14] We have since helped many leaders build stronger cultures, but working with our fearless and talented HBS colleagues to make the school better taught us the foundational truths about culture change.

We learned that any culture problem could be broken down and solved, even something as emotionally fraught as gender imbalances. We learned to honor a noble past while being unapologetic about the moral urgency of creating a better future. We learned that unlimited energy and creativity could be unleashed when an entire community steps up to lead. These are the requirements of any transformation—the pillars of the "Culture Change Playbook"—and we first learned them from HBS's courageous willingness to redefine *what is true*.

Step 1: Collect the devastating data

By 2010, it was clear that the school had a gender problem. The frustration of women on campus was high, and there were troubling demographic patterns in many of the school's performance indicators: women were underachieving men academically and were less satisfied with the MBA experience than their male peers. At this point, we did not have to collect any new data, but we did have to select the indicators to use to hold ourselves accountable for progress. We chose achievement and sentiment. If we could figure out how to move the needle on both, then we would know we were onto something.

Step 2: Keep it to yourself (for now)

The first thing we did with this data? Nothing, at least for the moment. Instead, the data informed the cultural vision of a new dean, renowned organizational behavior scholar Nitin Nohria. Nohria installed a diverse new leadership team, naming Frances head of the first-year curriculum, and charged us with ensuring that *all* students had the chance to thrive.[15] He empowered the team to make everything discussable and nothing untouchable, including shared assumptions and behaviors that had been in place for decades.

Step 3: Pilot a rigorous and optimistic way forward

We proceeded to pilot a wide range of changes that were anchored by a change in tone. When nine hundred or so first-year students piled into Burden Auditorium—a name with new resonance, as we all felt the weight of our obligation to the women on campus—for the dean's welcome address, they heard a different message from the one their predecessors had received. Rather than the jaunty, muscular "you've arrived" signaling that had characterized this ritual in the past, this class's first official gathering focused on the cornerstones of empowerment leadership: purpose, responsibility, accountability for the well-being of others.

The shift was threaded into classroom discussions, as well as a yearlong dialogue with the new class of MBA students. Frances met with students in a series of interactive discussions she hosted with the entire first-year class, ninety students at a time. In each of these discussions, she invited students to reframe their assumptions about leadership and their experience at HBS: "You've told us you're here

(continued)

to learn what leadership means. To us, it means taking care of each other. It means bringing out the best in each other. It means being accountable for your own choices but also the choices of the people you're leading. That will be your opportunity and obligation when you seek leadership roles beyond these walls, and it's the standard to which we'll hold you while you're a student here."

In addition to piloting a new tone, Frances and her colleagues were also willing to revisit the school's perhaps most sacred artifact: the case method. Demographic gaps in performance, it turned out, were driven primarily by differences in class participation. At the time, the school was getting feedback from industry that not all of its graduates were fully prepared for more amorphous leadership challenges like failing smartly and building inclusive teams. Companies that were thriving in the new, tech-infused economy were unleashing small teams to move fast and dream big in unpredictable environments. The school's traditional pedagogy was fostering many of the capabilities needed for this type of disruptive success, but not all of them.

These realities informed one of the biggest curricular experiments in the school's history: the introduction of the field method as a companion to the case method. The field method put students into small groups and tasked them with experiential work focused on leadership development, collaboration, and creativity. New teaching methods included personal reflection tools and feedback exercises in which students were expected to give each other honest assessments after meaningful group work. Faculty had been experimenting with these types of methods for years, but never at the scale of the entire first-year class. We introduced the field method to all first-year students, testing out a bold curriculum that pushed students to reflect continuously on how their behavior influenced others. In addition to the theoretical world of case problems, students now had to be accountable for who they were—and who they were not—in the unsparing context of reality.

These exploratory changes helped to make the MBA experience a better simulation of the real world of work. They also advanced the inclusion agenda by giving students more and varied ways to succeed. Students were now being rewarded for empathy, self-awareness, and their ability to handle the discomfort of vulnerability, just as they would be when they had to lead imperfect humans as imperfect humans themselves. They were immersed in the challenges of building trust, setting up other people to succeed, being a great teammate to someone who thinks differently from them. These were enduring truths of leadership, and their integration into the curriculum not only made women better, but also made everyone else better. They offered the entire student body a more rigorous, more optimistic way forward.

One additional by-product of these innovations, we believe, was that it became harder for students to dehumanize the people around them, even in small ways. Students got to know each other on a deeper level: in intimate one-on-one discussions, in the discomfort of solving problems with teammates you didn't choose, in the shared frustration of doing hard things together. Some of the incidents that had launched this cultural transformation, particularly the harassment of peers and faculty, felt almost inconceivable now.

The results? Gaps in performance between men and women closed completely within a *single* academic year. Gaps in satisfaction with

(*continued*)

the MBA program also closed, at the same dramatic rate, not only between men and women, but also between straight and LGBTQ+ students, and between US and international students—persistent disparities that had challenged the school since anyone could remember. At the end of the pilot year, the percentage of MBA students who reported high satisfaction with their experience jumped from roughly 50 percent to 70 percent. In subsequent years, those numbers climbed even higher. One student who came back to finish her degree after a leave of absence, one of the few to directly experience the before and after, described the school as "transformed" when she returned.

Step 4: Involve everyone in the solution

As the school moved to institutionalize many of these changes in the months and years that followed, something magical indeed happened: everyone got involved, even the students, improving our ideas in ways we never could have imagined. These improvements included exciting innovations to the FIELD curriculum, more inclusive algorithms for designing the student experience, even things like better childcare services for MBA students. They included more rigorous personal reflection work and a student-led Honor Code movement. Momentum increased dramatically in a community fueled by its own high standards and deep devotion, a community fully unleashed.

culture officers first. They're the VPs of product or sales or operations who mentally tack on "and culture" to whatever operating title they've earned. They're the leaders who quietly add culture to their job descriptions, wherever they happen to be in the hierarchy.

That's exactly the mentality that's made CEO Satya Nadella and his leadership team so effective at Microsoft. If you want to change an organization the size of Microsoft—filled with people you will rarely see, working in offices you will rarely enter—then you have no choice but to lead from a distance and, in particular, to lead through culture. When he became CEO in 2013, Nadella declared culture change his most important responsibility and dove headfirst into finding ways to get 130,000 employees to work differently in his absence.[16]

He started by changing their shared assumptions. Partnering closely with his chief people officer, Kathleen Hogan (remember her from chapter 4?), Nadella bet Microsoft's future on his ability to shift the company's beliefs about its most sensitive subjects: winning, losing, competition, diversity, even what it means to be part of a unified company. Together with the rest of the leadership team, they championed adoption of Carol Dweck's "growth mindset," focusing on behaviors this new mindset would unlock, including delighting customers, collaborating effectively, and fully embracing inclusion. They started by piloting new approaches across their own teams, and then found rigorous and optimistic ways to bring the rest of the company along.[17]

The short version of the story is that it worked. When Nadella started as CEO, the company's performance was stagnating. Five years later, in what has become one of the most exciting culture change stories of our lifetime, Microsoft's stock is at a record high, making it the most valuable company in the world as we write this. The entire organization is competing and innovating in unprecedented ways, and there's not a "wedge" in the company's strategy that hasn't grown. If you ask anyone, anywhere, what changed, their answer always begins with culture. In record time, the company's leadership team changed the way things are really done around Microsoft.

From the beginning, Nadella decided that creating and managing culture was the most important thing he would do as a leader. What would happen if you were to make the same decision? What kind of leader would you become? At the risk of overstepping our boundary as authors (why stop now?), we believe that the leader you would become is beyond anything you dreamed was possible. It's a leader who knows how to unleash not only individuals, but also whole organizations and beyond, a leader with the ability to change lives and institutions and even nations. We want to live in that world. We want our sons to grow up in that world. And our greatest hope in writing this book is that we've given you permission—and a few key guideposts—to continue your journey toward becoming that leader and empowering everyone around you.

GUT CHECK

Questions for Reflection

- ✓ Where does culture currently rank on your list of leadership priorities?

- ✓ If you could change anything about your firm's culture, what would it be? Which behaviors or underlying attitudes are getting in the way of your organization's success?

- ✓ Have any of your values or commitments to each other become empty or even "weaponized"? Are there values missing from your culture that are critical to your success?

- ✓ Which beliefs and behaviors have driven your own past successes as a leader? As you think about your *future* impact, do you need to evolve or let go of any of them?

- ✓ If you were to make organizational culture your most important priority as a leader, what would you do differently? Who or what would get more of your attention?

NOTES

Chapter 1

1. We introduced an earlier version of this definition in an article in *Harvard Business Review* (January–February 2011) that we wrote with our colleague Robin Ely titled "Stop Holding Yourself Back." Robin has been an important collaborator and inspiration to us personally and professionally. She makes us better.

2. David Gelles, "Stacy Brown-Philpot of TaskRabbit on Being a Black Woman in Silicon Valley," *New York Times*, July 13, 2018, https://www.nytimes.com/2018/07/13/business/stacy-brown-philpot-taskrabbit-corner-office.html.

3. Dave Lee, "On the Record: TaskRabbit's Stacy Brown-Philpot," *BBC News*, September 15, 2019, https://www.bbc.com/news/technology-49684677.

4. Reid Hoffman, "Keep Humans in the Equation—with TaskRabbit's Stacy Brown-Philpot," *Masters of Scale* (podcast), October 9, 2019, https://mastersofscale.com/stacy-brown-philpot-keep-humans-in-the-equation-masters-of-scale-podcast/.

5. "The Reid Hoffman Story—Make Everyone a Hero," WaitWhat, *Masters of Scale* (podcast), October 23, 2019, https://mastersofscale.com/reid-hoffman-make-everyone-a-hero/.

6. "Claire Hughes Johnson: How Stripe's COO Approaches Company Building," Lattice, YouTube, May 15, 2018, https://www.youtube.com/watch?v=vIHKzRub7ts.

7. Gen. Martin E. Dempsey, "Mission Command White Paper," Office of the Chairman of the Joint Chiefs of Staff, Washington, DC, April 2012.

8. Gallup, *State of the Global Workforce* (New York: Gallup Press, 2017).

Chapter 2

1. Susan Fowler, "Reflecting on One Very, Very Strange Year at Uber," *Susan Fowler* (blog), February 19, 2017, https://www.susanjfowler.com/blog/2017/2/19/reflecting-on-one-very-strange-year-at-uber.

2. Kara Swisher, ubiquitous journalist, entrepreneur, and conscience of the tech sector, was writing regularly about the urgent need for stronger leadership and accountability in the industry.

3. These ideas were explored in a TED talk Frances gave called "How to Build (and Rebuild) Trust" (TED Talk, TED2018, Vancouver, April 13, 2018).

4. Ethan S. Bernstein and Stephen Turban, "The Impact of the 'Open' Workspace on Human Collaboration," *Philosophical Transactions of the Royal Society B: Biological Sciences* (2018).

5. We want to thank Tien Larson for helping us to finally get this diagram right.

6. Yvon Chouinard, *Let My People Go Surfing: The Education of a Reluctant Businessman—Including 10 More Years of Business Unusual* (New York: Penguin Books, 2016), 1.

7. Jeff Beer, "How Patagonia Grows Every Time It Amplifies Its Social Mission," *Fast Company*, February 21, 2018, https://www.fastcompany.com /40525452/how-patagonia-grows-every-time-it-amplifies-its-social-mission.

8. Rose Marcario, "Patagonia CEO: This Is Why We're Suing President Trump," *Time*, December 6, 2017, https://time.com/5052617/patagonia-ceo-suing-donald-trump/.

9. Alana Semuels, "'Rampant Consumerism Is Not Attractive.' Patagonia Is Climbing to the Top—and Reimagining Capitalism Along the Way," *Time*, September 23, 2019, https://time.com/5684011/patagonia/.

10. Michael Corkery, "Walmart Says It Will Pay for Its Workers to Earn College Degrees," *New York Times*, May 30, 2018, https://www.nytimes .com/2018/05/30/business/walmart-college-tuition.html.

11. Paulo Freire, *Teachers as Cultural Workers: Letters to Those Who Dare to Teach* (Boulder, CO: Westview Press, 1998).

12. Victoria L. Brescoll and Eric Luis Uhlmann, "Can an Angry Woman Get Ahead? Status Conferral, Gender, and Expression of Emotion in the Workplace," *Psychological Science* 19, no. 3 (2008): 268–275, https://www.jstor .org/stable/40064922; Adia Harvey Wingfield, "The Modern Mammy and the Angry Black Man: African American Professionals' Experiences with Gendered Racism in the Workplace," *Race, Gender, & Class* 14, no. 1/2 (2007): 196–212, https://www.jstor.org/stable/41675204.

13. Amy Edmondson, *The Fearless Organization* (Hoboken, NJ: John Wiley & Sons, Inc., 2018).

14. Ibid., 45.

15. David Gigone and Reid Hastie, "The Common Knowledge Effect: Information Sharing and Group Judgment," *Journal of Personality and Social Psychology* 65, no. 5 (1993): 959–974.

16. Christina Pazzanese, "Teaching Uber instead of HBS Students," Business & Economy, *Harvard Gazette*, June 6, 2017, https://news.harvard .edu/gazette/story/2017/06/harvard-business-school-professor-to-tackle-ubers-controversial-internal-culture/.

17. Mike Isaac, "Inside Uber's Aggressive, Unrestrained Workplace Culture," Technology, *New York Times*, February 22, 2017, https://www .nytimes.com/2017/02/22/technology/uber-workplace-culture; Rani Molla, "Half of U.S. Uber Drivers Make Less Than $10 an Hour after Vehicle Expenses, According to New Study," *Vox*, October 2, 2018, https://www.vox.com/2018/10/2/17924628/ uber-drivers-make-hourly-expenses.

18. Leslie Hook, "Can Uber Ever Make Money?," Uber Technologies Inc., *Financial Times*, June 22, 2017, https://www.ft.com/content/09278d4e-579a-11e7-80b6-9bfa4c1f83d2.

19. Asma Khalid, "Uber Taps Harvard Business School's Frances Frei to Turn Company in Right Direction," WBUR, December 21, 2017, https://www .wbur.org/bostonomix/2017/12/21/uber-hires-frances-frei.

20. Mike Isaac, "How Uber Deceives the Authorities Worldwide," Technology, *New York Times*, March 3, 2017, https://www.nytimes.com/2017/03/03/ technology/uber-greyball-program-evade-authorities.

21. Kara Swisher, "Uber CEO Travis Kalanick Says the Company Has Hired Former Attorney General Eric Holder to Probe Allegations of Sexism," *Vox*, February 20, 2017, https://www.vox.com/2017/2/20/14677546/uber-ceo-travis-kalanick-eric-holder-memo.

22. Special Committee of the Board, "Covington Recommendations" (Google Doc, 2017), https://drive.google.com/file/d/0B1s08BdVqCgrUVM 4UHBpTGROLXM/view.

23. Sasha Lekach, "Uber Drivers Really Wanted In-app Tipping for a Reason: $600 Million Made in First Year," Tech, Mashable, June 21, 2018, https:// mashable.com/article/uber-tipping-600-million-first-year/.

24. Johana Bhuiyan, "Uber's Sleek New Product? Your Safety," *Vox*, September 6, 2018, https://www.vox.com/2018/9/6/17824294/uber-safety-product-features.

25. One of our favorite mindfulness evangelists is Dan Harris, ABC News correspondent and author of *10% Happier: How I Tamed the Voice in My Head, Reduced Stress without Losing My Edge, and Found Self-Help That Actually Works—A True Story* (New York: Harper Collins, 2014). It's a terrific book that chronicles Harris's journey from an on-air panic attack to no longer being at the mercy of negative thoughts.

26. Anne Morriss, Robin J. Ely, and Frances Frei, "Managing Yourself: Stop Holding Yourself Back," *Harvard Business Review*, January–February 2011.

27. Sheelah Kolhatkar, "At Uber, a New C.E.O. Shifts Gears," *New Yorker*, March 30, 2018, https://www.newyorker.com/magazine/2018/04/09/at-uber-a-new-ceo-shifts-gears; Dara Khosrowshahi, "A New Future for Uber and Grab in Southeast Asia," Uber Newsroom, March 26, 2018, https://www.uber.com/ newsroom/uber-grab/.

28. Frances spoke at length with Kara Swisher on the focus of the work and how the approach can be used at other companies. A full transcript of the

conversation can be found here: https://www.vox.com/2017/8/4/16092766/
transcript-uber-svp-leadership-diversity-women-culture-frances-frei-live-
onstage-recode-decode.

29. Leslie Hook, "Can Frances Frei Fix Uber?" Uber Technologies Inc.,
Financial Times, September 10, 2017, https://www.ft.com/content/a64de182-
93b2-11e7-a9e6-11d2f0ebb7f0.

30. Kara Swisher, "Uber's Culture Fixer, Frances Frei, Is Leaving the Company," *Vox*, February 27, 2018, https://www.vox.com/2018/2/27/17058348/
uber-culture-frances-frei-depart-travis-kalanick-dara-khosrowshahi-harvard-
business-school.

31. Mike Isaac, "Uber Sells Stake to SoftBank, Valuing Ride-Hailing Giant
at $48 Billion," Technology, *New York Times*, December 28, 2017, https://www
.nytimes.com/2017/12/28/technology/uber-softbank-stake.htm.

Chapter 3

1. We are incredibly grateful to the amazing Professor Emma Dench of Harvard University for introducing us to Valerius Maximus and many of her other
long-departed friends. Emma and Frances co-taught a course called "Leadership
Lessons from Ancient Rome" to MBA students in the fall of 2015. The experience
profoundly changed the way we think about past and present, as well as their
intimate connections to each other. This chapter attempts to honor that gift.

2. Valerius Maximus, *Memorable Doings and Sayings, Volume II: Books
6–9*, ed. D. R. Shackleton Bailey (Cambridge, MA: Harvard University
Press, 2000).

3. Ibid., 65.

4. Kevin Kelleher, "AMD's 50-Year Tug-of-War with Intel Just Took an
Interesting Turn," *Fortune*, May 29, 2019, https://fortune.com/2019/05/28/amd-
intel-ryzen/.

5. Lydia Dishman, "How This CEO Avoided the Glass Cliff and Turned
around an 'Uninvestable' Company," *Fast Company*, September 10, 2018,
https://www.fastcompany.com/90229663/how-amds-ceo-lisa-su-managed-to-
turn-the-tech-company-around.

6. We've been handing out laminated cards of this framework to our students for the last fifteen years. In almost every corner of the planet, we've had the
awesome experience of running into someone who pulled out one of these cards,
sometimes torn and yellowed after years of being stuffed into a wallet, and told us
how the ideas made a difference in their lives. We live for these moments.

7. Our friend Amy Edmondson offers a similar framework, derived from
her groundbreaking work on psychological safety, in her terrific book, *The
Fearless Organization*. Here, she describes the optimal performance state of high
standards and high psychological safety.

8. "Peru: Journey to Self-Reliance FY 2019 Country Roadmap," USAID,
https://selfreliance.usaid.gov/country/peru.

9. Maximus, *Memorable Doings and Sayings*, 82.

10. Ibid., 84.

11. Carol Dweck, *Mindset: The New Psychology of Success* (New York: Random House, 2006), 71–72.

12. Marcus Buckingham and Ashley Goodall, "The Feedback Fallacy," *Harvard Business Review*, March–April 2019.

13. Walter Isaacson, "The Real Leadership Lessons of Steve Jobs," *Harvard Business Review*, April 2012, https://hbr.org/2012/04/the-real-leadership-lessons-of-steve-jobs.

14. Ibid.

15. Jolie Kerr, "How to Talk to People, According to Terry Gross," *New York Times*, November 17, 2018, https://www.nytimes.com/2018/11/17/style/self-care/terry-gross-conversation-advice.html.

Chapter 4

1. There is too much good work in this area to properly honor, but thinkers and scholars who have inspired us recently include Modupe Akinola, Melinda Gates (yes, that Melinda Gates), Boris Groysberg, Denise Lewin Lloyd, Anthony Mayo, Lauren Rivera, and Laura Morgan Roberts. For the intellectual adventure of a lifetime, start with their work on race and gender equity.

2. AnitaB.org, "Homepage," https://ghc.anitab.org.

3. Pamella de Leon, "Entrepreneur Middle East's Achieving Women 2019: Cammie Dunaway, Chief Marketing Officer, Duolingo," *Entrepreneur*, September 22, 2019, https://www.entrepreneur.com/article/339699.

4. Maureen Farrell et al., "The Fall of WeWork: How a Startup Darling Came Unglued," *Wall Street Journal*, October 24, 2019, https://www.wsj.com/articles/the-fall-of-wework-how-a-startup-darling-came-unglued-11571946003.

5. TED, "The TED Interview: Frances Frei's Three Pillars of Leadership," *A TED Original Podcast*, Podcast audio, November 2019, https://www.ted.com/talks/the_ted_interview_frances_frei_s_three_pillars_of_leadership.

6. Two organizations doing great work on women's representation in leadership—both applied research and functional support—are the Stanford's VMware Women's Leadership Innovation Lab and LeanIn.Org. A practical first step is to sign up for their newsletters.

7. Alex Coop, "Leaders in Davos Stress Diversity and Inclusion of Women in Tech," IT Business, January 26, 2018, https://www.itbusiness.ca/news/leaders-in-davos-stress-diversity-and-inclusion-of-women-in-tech/98784.

8. Alison M. Konrad, Vicki Kramer, and Sumru Erkut, "Critical Mass: The Impact of Three or More Women on Corporate Boards," *Organizational Dynamics* 37, no. 2 (2008): 145–164.

9. Paul Solman, "How Xerox Became a Leader in Diversity—and Why That's Good for Business," *PBS News Hour*, September 15, 2014, https://www.pbs.org/newshour/economy/xerox-employees-arent-carbon-copies.

10. Much of the credit for this work goes to Matt Jahansouz, who assembled a team from diverse industries and life experiences at a pace required of a high-growth company.

11. Dave Itzkoff, "Samantha Bee Prepares to Debut 'Full Frontal,'"
New York Times, January 6, 2016, https://www.nytimes.com/2016/01/10/arts/television/samantha-bee-prepares-to-break-up-late-night-tvs-boys-club.html.

12. Ibid.

13. National Public Radio (NPR), "Only 3 Minority Head Coaches Remain in the NFL Ahead of Post-Season Play," https://www.npr.org/2019/01/04/682350052/only-3-minority-head-coaches-remain-in-the-nfl-ahead-of-post-season-play.

14. Catherine E. Harnois and João L. Bastos, "Discrimination, Harassment, and Gendered Health Inequalities: Do Perceptions of Workplace Mistreatment Contribute to the Gender Gap in Self-reported Health?" *Journal of Health and Social Behavior* 59, no. 2 (2018): 283–299.

15. Countless resources are available to support you in the creation of safe and healthy workplaces. As a starting point, we like the EEOC's online summary of "promising practices": https://www.eeoc.gov/eeoc/publications/promising-practices.cfm.

16. Amy Edmondson, *The Fearless Organization* (Hoboken, NJ: John Wiley & Sons, Inc., 2019), xvi.

17. Amy Elisa Jackson, "Why Salesforce's New Equality Chief Is Thinking Beyond Diversity," *Fast Company*, March 20, 2017, https://www.fastcompany.com/3069082/why-salesforces-new-equality-chief-is-thinking-beyond-diversity.

18. Zing Tsjeng, "Teens These Days Are Queer AF, New Study Says," *Vice*, March 10, 2016, https://www.vice.com/en_us/article/kb4dvz/teens-these-days-are-queer-af-new-study-says.

19. "Curriculum," The Safe Zone Project, https://thesafezoneproject.com/curriculum/.

20. Shalayne Pulia, "Meet Deirdre O'Brien, the Apple Executive Bringing a Human Touch to the Tech Giant," *InStyle*, November 7, 2019, https://www.instyle.com/celebrity/deirdre-obrien-apple-badass-women.

21. Shana Lebowitz, "Microsoft's HR Chief Reveals How CEO Satya Nadella Is Pushing to Make Company Culture a Priority, the Mindset She Looks for in Job Candidates, and Why Individual Success Doesn't Matter as Much as It Used To," *Business Insider*, August 16, 2019, https://www.businessinsider.com/microsoft-hr-chief-kathleen-hogan-company-culture-change-satya-nadella-2019-8.

22. Professor Frank Flynn, now at Stanford University, developed this experiment while he was teaching at Columbia, building on the original "Heidi Roizen" case (Kathleen L. McGinn and Nicole Tempest, "Heidi Roizen," Case 800-228 [Boston: Harvard Business School, 2000; revised 2010.].) It's beautiful pedagogy.

23. Rachel Bachman, "U.S. Women's Soccer Games Outearned Men's Games," *Wall Street Journal*, June 17, 2019, https://www.wsj.com/articles/u-s-womens-soccer-games-out-earned-mens-games-11560765600.

24. John A. Byrne, "Harvard B-school Dean Offers Unusual Apology," *Fortune*, January 29, 2014, https://fortune.com/2014/01/29/harvard-b-school-dean-offers-unusual-apology.

Chapter 5

1. In addition to the privilege of working side by side with some of the world's most effective strategic operators, a number of experiences have profoundly influenced our understanding of strategy. Frances taught the required Strategy course at HBS, which uses as its intellectual foundation the work of Michael Porter, Jan Rivkin, Bharat Anand, and many other amazing faculty from the strategy unit at Harvard Business School. In addition, Anne spent a number of years working with the OTF Group, a global consulting firm that applied Michael Porter's ideas and frameworks to the challenge of building competitiveness in emerging economies.

2. Frances Frei and Anne Morriss, *Uncommon Service: How to Win by Putting Customers at the Core of Your Business* (Boston: Harvard Business Review Press, 2012).

3. A visualization tool introduced to us by our colleague Jan Rivkin, attribute maps allow you to measure firm performance relative to competitor performance based on a market segment's ranking of key product features.

4. James L. Heskett, "Southwest Airlines 2002: An Industry under Siege," Case 803-133 (Boston: Harvard Business School, 2003); and Frances X. Frei and Corey B. Hajim, "Rapid Rewards at Southwest Airlines," Case 602-065 (Boston: Harvard Business School, 2001; revised 2004).

5. We originally heard this story from the great Earl Sasser, Baker Foundation Professor at Harvard Business School, in December 2006. It is retold in more detail in Frei and Morriss, *Uncommon Service*.

6. Patty Azzarello, *Rise: 3 Practical Steps for Advancing Your Career, Standing Out as a Leader, and Liking Your Life* (New York: Ten Speed Press, 2012).

7. Many of the ideas in this section are also described in "Better, Simpler Strategy," a pamphlet Frances coauthored with Felix Oberholzer-Gee (Frances X. Frei and Felix Oberholzer-Gee, "Better, Simpler Strategy," Baker Library, Boston, September 2017). Felix is a friend and colleague who understands the principles of strategy deeply and describes them clearly and elegantly. His fantastic book, *Value-based Strategy: A Guide to Understanding Exceptional Performance*, is forthcoming.

8. This framework is an illustration of value-based strategy, an approach to strategic management that builds on the foundational work of Michael Porter, Adam Brandenburger, and Harbone Stuart.

9. David Yoffie and Eric Baldwin, "Apple Inc. in 2015," Case 715-456 (Boston: Harvard Business School, 2015).

10. Tim O'Reilly, *WTF: What's the Future and Why It's Up to Us* (New York: Harper Business, 2017).

11. Tony Hsieh, *Delivering Happiness* (New York: Grand Central Publishing, 2010), 185–186.

12. Ibid., 187–188.

13. Zeynep Ton, *The Good Jobs Strategy: How the Smartest Companies Invest in Employees to Lower Costs and Boost Profits* (New York: Houghton Mifflin, 2014).

14. QuikTrip, "QuikTrip Opens 800th Store, Celebrates Huge Growth Milestone in Its 60-Year History," *QuikTrip News*, April 3, 2019, https://www.quiktrip.com/About/News/quiktrip-opens-800th-store-celebrates-huge-growth-milestone-in-its-60-year-history.

15. Joe Nocera, "The Good Jobs Strategy," *New York Times*, July 7, 2015. https://www.nytimes.com/2015/07/07/opinion/joe-nocera-the-good-jobs-strategy.html.

16. Neil Irwin, "Maybe We're Not All Going to Be Gig Economy Workers after All," *New York Times*, September 15, 2019, https://www.nytimes.com/2019/09/15/upshot/gig-economy-limits-labor-market-uber-california.html.

17. David Gelles, "Stacy Brown-Philpot of TaskRabbit on Being a Black Woman in Silicon Valley," *New York Times*, July 13, 2018, https://www.nytimes.com/2018/07/13/business/stacy-brown-philpot-taskrabbit-corner-office.html.

18. David Lee, "On the Record: TaskRabbit's Stacy Brown-Philpot," *BBC News*, September 15, 2019, https://www.bbc.com/news/technology-49684677.

19. Casey Newton, "TaskRabbit Is Blowing Up Its Business Model and Becoming the Uber for Everything," The Verge, June 17, 2014, https://www.theverge.com/2014/6/17/5816254/taskrabbit-blows-up-its-auction-house-to-offer-services-on-demand.

20. Lee, "On the Record: TaskRabbit's Stacy Brown-Philpot."

21. James K. Willcox, "Cable TV Fees Continue to Climb," *Consumer Reports*, October 15, 2019, https://www.consumerreports.org/tv-service/cable-tv-fees/.

22. Steven J. Spear and H. Kent Bowen, "Decoding the DNA of the Toyota Production System," *Harvard Business Review*, September 1, 1999.

23. Shawn Achor et al., "9 Out of 10 People Are Willing to Earn Less Money to Do More-Meaningful Work," *Harvard Business Review*, November 6, 2018.

24. Brittain Ladd, "Amazon CEO Jeff Bezos Believes This Is the Best Way to Run Meetings," *Observer*, June 10, 2019, https://observer.com/2019/06/amazon-ceo-jeff-bezos-meetings-success-strategy/.

25. "Amazon CEO Jeff Bezos: It Is Always Day One," YouTube, 2018, https://www.youtube.com/watch?v=KPbKeNghRYE.

26. We are paraphrasing one of Anne's writing teachers, the wonderful Rhoda Flaxman. Flaxman taught British and American Literature at Brown

University, where she also directed Brown's writing-across-the curriculum program and published on Victorian literature.

27. Jan Carlzon, *Moments of Truth* (New York: HarperBusiness, 1987).

28. Ibid., 88.

29. Elizabeth Dunn, "Momofuku's Secret Sauce: A 30-Year-Old C.E.O.," *New York Times*, August 16, 2019, https://www.nytimes.com/2019/08/16/business/momofuku-ceo-marguerite-mariscal.html.

30. Tsedal Neeley, *The Language of Global Success: How a Common Tongue Transforms Multinational Organizations* (Princeton, NJ: Princeton University Press, 2017).

Chapter 6

1. Michael Basch, *Customer Culture: How FedEx and Other Great Companies Put the Customer First Every Day* (Upper Saddle River, NJ: Prentice Hall PTR, 2003), 8.

2. Edgar H. Schein, *Organizational Culture and Leadership* (San Francisco: Jossey-Boss, 1991).

3. Norm Brodsky, "Learning from JetBlue," *Inc.*, March 1, 2004.

4. Schein, *Organizational Culture and Leadership*, 2.

5. Nancy Hass, "And the Award for the Next HBO Goes To . . . ," *GQ*, January 29, 2013, https://www.gq.com/story/netflix-founder-reed-hastings-house-of-cards-arrested-development.

6. McCord tells the complete story herself in her terrific book, *Powerful: Building a Culture of Freedom and Responsibility* (USA: Silicon Guild, 2017).

7. Mike Isaac, *Super Pumped: The Battle for Uber* (New York: W.W. Norton & Company, Inc., 2019), 265.

8. Anyone who cares about getting culture right should read Susan Fowler, *Whistleblower: My Journey to Silicon Valley and Fight for Justice at Uber* (New York: Viking, 2020).

9. We admire the practices of world-class leadership coaches like Jerry Colonna, who has dedicated his career to helping leaders disrupt the path from personal history to company dysfunction. He wrote a fantastic book about the experience titled *Reboot: Leadership and the Art of Growing Up* (New York: Harper Business, 2019).

10. Dara Khosrowshahi, "Uber's New Cultural Norms," LinkedIn (blog), November 7, 2017, https://www.linkedin.com/pulse/ubers-new-cultural-norms-dara-khosrowshahi/.

11. Cecilia D'Anastasio, "Inside the Culture of Sexism at Riot Games," *Kotaku*, August 7, 2018, https://kotaku.com/inside-the-culture-of-sexism-at-riot-games-1828165483.

12. Riot Games, "Our First Steps Forward," News, Riot website, August 29, 2018, https://www.riotgames.com/en/who-we-are/our-first-steps-forward.

13. Riot internal survey data, collected November 2019.

14. Jerry Useem, "Harvard Business School's 'Woman Problem,'" *Inc.*, June 1, 1998, https://www.inc.com/magazine/19980601/940.html.

15. The team included Youngme Moon as chair of the MBA Program, Tom Eisenmann as head of the MBA Elective Curriculum (second year), and Robin Ely as the leader of culture and community.

16. Satya Nadella, Greg Shaw, and Jill Tracie Nichols, *Hit Refresh: The Quest to Rediscover Microsoft's Soul and Imagine a Better Future for Everyone* (New York: HarperBusiness, 2017).

17. Ibid, 4–11, 80–95.

INDEX

DISCLOSURES

Many of the insights and examples we use are derived from our experiences working with specific organizations. Both individually and in association with firms we have founded, including The Morriss Group, we have actively advised many of the companies in this book, including Riot Games, Uber, and WeWork. In addition, Frances has taught extensively in Harvard Business School's Executive Education program and in private executive education settings, where she has engaged with leaders from many of the companies we discuss. Finally, some of the companies we mention are clients of The Leadership Consortium (TLC), an organization we started, where Anne currently serves as Executive Founder. These firms have sent high-potential leaders through TLC's Leaders Program, which is focused primarily on helping women and people of color prepare for senior leadership roles.

ACKNOWLEDGMENTS

We are finishing this project with all kinds of emotions: relief at getting to this point, resolve to do more, regret for what we inevitably left out. Those feelings are overpowered by a deep sense of gratitude for the people who helped us bring the book to life.

First, we are deeply thankful for the talent and hard work of our intrepid research team, anchored by Katie Boland and Francesca Ely-Spence. They made the book better in their righteous pursuit of integrity and truth.

The fantastic team at Harvard Business Review Press protected and nurtured the ideas in this book from the very beginning. We are particularly grateful to Melinda Merino, our visionary editor, who led us through the process with skill, clarity, patience, and an infectious sense of possibility.

Our early readers made a difference, at the points when we most needed to be saved from ourselves. They include Emmy Berning, Emma Dench, Carlos Flores, Tsedal Neeley, Sarah Schutz, Melissa Statires, and Libbie Thacker. David A. Preiss also contributed his considerable design talent to a number of the figures in the book.

Our friends and colleagues at Harvard Business School have been on this adventure with us for decades, both personally and professionally. We are particularly thankful for the friendship, leadership, and intellectual courage of Amy Edmondson, Robin Ely, Jan

Hammond, Youngme Moon, and Nitin Nohria. Where possible, we have tried to honor the way their ideas have shaped us, but we recognize that this is an impossible task, given their outsized influence. Know that Youngme is mentioned far less in the book than the reality of her impact on our lives and the institutions we inhabit. Her leadership in HBS's cultural turnaround, in particular, has deeply influenced our own ambition and belief in what's possible.

We are grateful to our incredible sons, Alec and Ben, who inspired, supported, and tolerated us throughout the writing of this book. Know, always, that you are deeply loved. To the rest of our dear family and friends, thank you for helping us create space for this project—and for understanding when it required us to disappear. We also want to say that we have a wonderful support team at home that makes it possible for us to be parents to our children and also active in the world. We could not do any of this without you.

Countless writers have influenced us, through their craft and vision, and also as fearless artists who continue to demand an audience, some of them from the great beyond. Many times, in the writing of this book, we thought about their example and impact. This presumptuous shortlist includes but is not limited to Rachel Held Evans, Clarice Lispector, Toni Morrison, our dear friend Curtis Sittenfeld, Lucian Truscott, and Jeanette Winterson.

Finally, to all of the extraordinary leaders we've had the privilege of studying, only some of whom made it onto these pages: this book is not only for you, but also by you and in many ways *of* you. We are on the long list of people empowered by your courage, wisdom, and willingness to share your leadership path with us.

ABOUT THE AUTHORS

FRANCES FREI is a professor at Harvard Business School. Her research investigates how leaders create the context for organizations and individuals to thrive by designing for excellence in strategy, operations, and culture. Frei regularly works with companies embarking on large-scale change and organizational transformation, including embracing diversity and inclusion as a lever for improved performance. In 2017 she served as Uber's first Senior Vice President of Leadership and Strategy to help the company navigate its very public crisis in leadership and culture.

ANNE MORRISS is a highly sought-after leadership coach and the Executive Founder of The Leadership Consortium, a first-of-its-kind leadership accelerator that works to help more and varied leaders thrive. She has spent the last twenty years building and leading mission-driven enterprises, serving most recently as CEO and founder of GenePeeks. Morriss started her career in Latin America, where she worked to support the development of local leaders. Her collaborators have ranged from early-stage tech founders to *Fortune* 50 executives to public-sector leaders building national competitiveness.

Frei and Morriss are also the authors of *Uncommon Service: How to Win by Putting Customers at the Core of Your Business.*